Mirror Mirror Off The Wall

Mirror Mirror Off The Wall

✦

A Personal Experience of Intertwined Obsessive/Compulsive Spectrum Disorders: Body Dysmorphic Disorder and Trichotillomania

By Jenifer Wolf

Writers Club Press
New York Lincoln Shanghai

Mirror Mirror Off The Wall
A Personal Experience of Intertwined Obsessive/Compulsive Spectrum Disorders: Body Dysmorphic Disorder and Trichotillomania

Writers Club Press
an imprint of iUniverse, Inc.

For information address:
iUniverse, Inc.
2021 Pine Lake Road, Suite 100
Lincoln, NE 68512
www.iuniverse.com

The names of members of support groups have been changed, to protect their identities.

ISBN: 0-595-26254-6

Printed in the United States of America

To My Mother

Acknowledgements

Thanks to my editor, Bob Davis, for his excellent work on my manuscript.

Thanks to Sharon Brandt for her great cover design.

Thanks to my friend, Lee Williams, for her many apt suggestions for improving the manuscript.

Thanks to my friend and onetime co-author, Maryanne Raphael for her inspiration and encouragement.

Thanks to my son, Alex Wolf for his dogged insistence that I complete this project.

Finally, thanks to all those who have helped me to understand and cope with the Obsessive Compulsive Spectrum Disorders, which have plagued me for most of my life.

Contents

In 1989, after 33 years of succumbing to a weird, incomprehensible Disorder, I became aware that my Disorder had a name, and that I was not the only person who suffered from it. I learned that I had Trichotillomania, an Obsessive/Compulsive Spectrum Disorder. At the same time, I learned that there were treatments for my Disorder.

People with Trichotillomania usually pull hair out with their fingers, most frequently the hair on the head or eye lashes, although the hair pulling focus can be any site on the body. I had a variation, which was that I always used implements, tweezers or scissors.

During the late '80s, I was seeing a psychotherapist, who, unfortunately was not aware of Obsessive/Compulsive Disorder or Obsessive/Compulsive Spectrum Disorders like Trichotillomania. She simply attributed my dipilatory proclivities to low self-esteem, which certainly didn't enhance my self-esteem.

After discovering what my problem was, and realizing that my therapist was unaware of its nature, I felt that a support group might offer the best opportunity for understanding and coping with my Disorder. After a 2 year search, I finally found an Obsessive/Compulsive Anonymous group.

the underlying theme of both was that what belonged to me was being stolen from me. What was being stolen from me and how could I prevent it in the future?

Rita had suggested, "grooming behaviors" as a topic, since all of as at that
meeting (including two new member named Debbie and Sarah) had
compulsive, repetitive grooming behaviors. We all agreed that these behaviors
provoked more anxiety than they alleviated.

I found that an SSRI can be helpful, but a lot of the work was still up to me.

Where I am now with respect to my Disorder.

Preface

Any clinician who has ever worked closely with an individual suffering from an Obsessive/Compulsive Spectrum Disorder quickly learns what it truly means to be courageous. For those suffering from these illnesses, hours turn into days, weeks, months and sometimes years in a constant search for that all too elusive perfection that promises relief, but can never be achieved. All the while the individual is plagued with anxiety, at times, so severe that his or her social and occupational functioning is ground to a halt. Obsessive/Compulsive Disorder and its related Disorders are estimated to affect approximately 2-3% of the United States population, compelling them to endlessly check, wash, order, cut, organize, ruminate or simply collect. For some, these Disorders become so overwhelming that there is little time for the simplest of pleasures as its "voice" pervades one's consciousness.

Of course, all hope is not lost, since psycho pharmacology and psychotherapy have teamed up, if not to eliminate the Disorder, then, at least, to render its attacks feeble. Selective Serotonin Re-uptake Inhibitors along with Cognitive/Behavioral Therapy have offered sufferers of Obsessive/Compulsive Disorder and Obsessive/Compulsive Spectrum Disorders weapons with which to effectively challenge and ameliorate the anxiety which binds them. In the pages that follow you will read about the journey of one woman whose suffering with Trichotillomania and Body Dysmorphic Disorder waxed and waned until, through her persistence and consistency, she came upon the combination of treatments that made it possible for her to prevail. It epitomizes the courage referred to in the opening sentence of this introduction.

David Miller, Ph.D.—July 2002

About the Foreword

Because Obsessive/Compulsive Disorder and Obsessive/Compulsive Spectrum Disorders impact not only the individual with these Disorders, but also the families, significant others and close friends of such individuals, my son Alex has written an unflinching forward, which I believe will resonate with other children of parents with OCD and OCSDs.

Foreword

As a child in the late 60s and 70s, like all kids living with a parent afflicted by an intractable mental illness, my life was dramatically affected by something that was a mystery to me. What I recall is that my mother would disappear into the bathroom for endless hours. I have distinct memories of mounds of black-covered towels and sheets and sheets of black-covered toilet paper. As a young boy I was not aware of what this soot-like covering was. I just remember that when my mother would finally emerge from the bathroom, she looked strangely drawn and preoccupied. It was as if there was some bizarre alchemy which kept my mother locked in the grips of the bathroom mirror for countless hours, which to me, as a child, felt like eternity.

Now, I can see that I experienced my mother's preoccupation as abandonment. She was unreachable during these periods. I remember her saying, "just one minute…," as her voice trailed off into a dead silence of minutes spanning into hours.

I also was embarrassed when I accompanied her to family events, hours after they had begun. For example, we showed up at my brother Jonathan's Bar Mitzvah just as the ceremony was concluding. I also recall arriving at a family friend's Thanksgiving celebration long after the feast had been consumed. On these and other occasions, my mother was greeted with expressions of anger and outrage. She had no explanation for her lateness, and being a child who certainly had no concept of my mother's aberrant psychology, I couldn't fathom her behavior. The consequence for me was frustration and a feeling of deep deprivation. Events that I happily anticipated would become an agony of waiting for her to appear from behind the bathroom door.

In retrospect, I realize that my mother was suffering from an untreated mental illness, which was a source of trauma for me.

Today, I am proud of my mother for all the strides she has made in combating her life-long illness. This book is a testament to the degree to which she has recovered, as well as to her commitment to help others in their personal struggle against mental illness.

Alex Wolf—August, 2002

Introduction

Mirror Mirror Off The Wall is about my almost life-long experience of a variety of Obsessive/Compulsive Spectrum Disorders, as well as some classic Obsessive/Compulsive symptoms. My purpose in writing this memoir is to exorcise my own demons and, in so doing, to help others with Obsessive/Compulsive Disorder (OCD) and Obsessive/Compulsive Spectrum Disorders (OCSDs) to better understand and cope with what they are going through.

I emphatically am not implying that books and articles on these subjects by professionals are lacking in importance. In fact, the professional literature, much of which is alluded to in this volume, has been invaluable to me and I strongly advise anyone with these Disorders to avail themselves of it.

Although research into OCD and OCSDs had been going on since the early 1970s, it was not until the late 1980s and early 1990s that, through the mass media, the general public began to be aware of these Disorders. And for me, just knowing that I wasn't alone with what felt like insanity provoked a major shift in my outlook. I began, gradually, to emerge from my self-imposed veil of secrecy. Knowing that there were others with Disorders similar to mine, made me seek out a support group before the possibility of going into therapy had even occurred to me. That was because of greatest importance to me after first encountering an article about my Disorder in 1989 wasn't a cure or even a diminution of symptoms. Rather, it was the acceptance and empathy of fellow sufferers.

After having been in a support group for several months, I did decide to get professional help, largely because people in my support group had told me that although there was no cure for OCD or

OCSDs, Cognitive/Behavioral Therapy in tandem with one of a group of anti-depressants called Selective Serotonin Re-uptake Inhibitors (SSRIs) could make a vast difference in both the intensity of the Disorder and the amount of time that one was enmeshed in it. My support group members warned that these stratagems didn't work for everyone, but that they were, at the very least, worth a serious commitment over a period of months.

The people in my group were right on both counts: there is no cure for OCD or OCSDs, but the right combination of drugs and therapy can make an enormous difference in the quality of life of those who suffer with Obsessive/Compulsive Disorder and Obsessive/Compulsive Spectrum Disorders.

This is the story of how my all-consuming Obsessions and Compulsions became progressively more manageable. And though they still entice me on a daily basis and sometimes succeed for short periods, they no longer run my life; I do.

Jenifer Wolf—August, 2002

Revelation

In March of 1989, I learned that the bizarre ritual which had held me in thrall for 33 years had a name. And for the first time in all that time, I knew that there were other people with equally strange and unrelenting Compulsions.

My friend Joel had brought me a story he'd cut from the *Words* section of *People Magazine*. It was an interview with Dr. Judith Rappoport, a pioneer in the study and treatment of what she termed Obsessive/Compulsive Disorder. She said that the Compulsions were senseless rituals, performed over and over again, with full realization of how senseless they were. Dr. Rappoport analogized Obsessive/Compulsive Disorder (OCD) to a hiccup of the mind.

Trichotillomania

All of the foregoing seemed to relate to my problem. What made me certain that this article referred to my apparently irresistible urge to cut both my eye lashes and the hair on my head, was the section that Joel had highlighted in clear yellow. It said, "We have (also) treated a small group of women with the Compulsion to pull out their hair, one strand at a time. Some are bald and wear wigs; others have no brows or lashes."

True, pulling and cutting aren't identical, but the weird mental blip that gripped me had actually begun with pulling out my lashes with tweezers. At some point, I'd switched to cutting the lashes, and later, I alternated between cutting my lashes and cutting or shaving the hair on my head. And, like all of the people described by Dr. Rappoport, I knew that what I was doing was nuts, but I got lost in it and couldn't stop.

A week later Joel returned and gave me a neatly torn piece of paper. On it, he'd written one seven-syllable word, "Trichotillomania," which means regularly pulling out the hair on one's head, or on any other site on one's body. I wondered about the origin of this strange word. I discovered that it's derived from three Greek words: 'trich', which means 'hair'; 'tillo', which means 'pull'; and 'mania'; which means 'abnormal love'. I've noticed that most of the people I've met, who have Trichotillomania, hate the word, probably because of the "mania" part. I find the sound of "Trichotillomania" amusing. And the fact that the Disorder has been devastating for me, doesn't prevent me from enjoying a giggle at its name.

I tweezed or cut my lashes inches from a mirror, not seeing my face whole, only individual lashes and the section of lid that they were embedded in. It was a breathless, painstaking activity. It was also sequestered and secretive. I was a prisoner of the bathroom for three to eight hours each day, in perpetual fear that someone would discover what I was doing there. In contrast, cutting the hair on my head was, at least initially, an exuberantly destructive act. But it immediately became incorporated into the existing Obsessive/Compulsive structure, alternating with lash cutting. The new variation was often more casual, at least to begin with, than the established one. It could begin while I was on the phone or watching TV. Initially, I could check by touch to see which hairs "needed to be cut." Eventually, though, I always ended up inches from the bathroom mirror, endlessly fixated. As an activity, there isn't a lot of difference between cutting lashes and cutting hair on the head. However, baldness is a lot more noticeable than lashlessness, so this later variation on a theme ultimately forced my Disorder into the open. It made my life more difficult, but, at the same time, it increased my chances of attracting useful information of the sort I'd received from Joel.

Insight Oriented Therapy

At the apogee of my bald period, I was seeing a therapist, who never truly seemed to comprehend the nature of my problem, although I'd tried hard to convey it. She saw my inability to stop cutting my hair as a symptom of low self-esteem, an evaluation which didn't seem to me an adequate explanation of the need to engage in such a strange and specific behavior time and time again, a behavior which I recognized as being self-destructive, except when I was actively engaged in it. My gut feeling was that, although both my tendency to evaluate myself negatively and the pervasiveness of my uncontrollable urge to cut waxed and waned, there wasn't a direct correlation between the two phenomena. I finally left the therapist, because no progress was being made with respect to my Obsession with the appearance of my lashes and hair, and my Compulsion to rectify even the most minute irregularities by cutting, cutting, cutting.

Search For A Support Group

After I read the interview with Judith Rappoport, my feeling about the relationship between my self-esteem and my Compulsion seemed to make sense: The Compulsion was as much a cause as a result of self-doubt. And, I thought, that since my therapist, who seemed to keep up with the current literature in clinical psychology, hadn't understood the nature of my problem, my best chance of gaining insight into my Disorder was from other people who had it.

My search for an Obsessive/Compulsive or Trichotillomania support group was long and frustrating. I would hear about a group, and, as soon as I approached it, I would learn that it had disbanded. My perception was that there was this group that I needed to be in that kept eluding me. With hindsight, I can see that the chase certainly enhanced my appreciation of the experience I eventually had, when I began to attend weekly meetings of Obsessive/Compulsive Anonymous.

Obsessive Compulsive Anonymous

The Obsessive Compulsive Anonymous "fellowship," as the support groups based on Alcoholics Anonymous are called, had been around for about two years, but this particular meeting was new. My friend Robin, who chaired another meeting on the same floor and was familiar with my (thus far) thwarted attempt to find an Obsessive/Compulsive support group, had seen an announcement on the bulletin board and informed me about it excitedly. I liked the idea of going to a group that was just getting started.

The chairperson of the OCA group, Rhonda, was a 12-step veteran and booster. I found her rather too controlling in the role of moderator, but a source of inspiration, when she recounted her experience of OCD. She said that at age seven she had begun compulsively performing rituals involving checking on household appliances over and over again. The particulars of both her family background and her Disorder were very different from mine. But there was also an important similarity: parental expectations that we would excel, and consequent fear of disappointing those expectations.

Rhonda said that her ritual checking was not, at present, a regular feature of her life, though it still cropped up from time to time, when she was particularly anxious. She attributed the immense improvement in her condition to the OCA meetings, to a supportive marriage, and to making greater demands of herself.

I agreed that marriage, or simply living with others, tends to limit the pervasiveness of the Compulsive behavior. It had done so in my case. But cohabitation had also created more guilt about the Compulsions, as well as adding to the original Obsessive/Compulsive Disorder a fear of discovery and all of the lies, subterfuges, and evasions which that fear entailed. What made all the difference in Rhonda's case was that her husband knew about her Disorder and was an ally in her struggle against it, not an adversary or judge from whom the Disorder had to be kept secret.

Rhonda's other solution, making more demands of herself, had, for me, usually been self-defeating. Giving myself injunctions, musts and shoulds has tended to amplify my anxiety, leading to an increase in the duration and intensity of my Compulsions. What has been effective in curtailing Compulsive episodes was to give myself activities, which I could anticipate with pleasure. My former therapist, Barbara, had been correct when she said I needed to do more things that were fun.

Actually, I could not understand how activities which give me intense pleasure, like going to movies and museums, reading books and dancing could simply recede from my consciousness for weeks, even months at a time. I wasn't intentionally punishing myself, but that was certainly the effect of my neglect of those pursuits which inspire new perspectives and renewed energies. And, not infrequently, it would take me a week to realize that I was sliding into despondency, because the dust I'd allowed to accumulate was irritating my sinuses. But worse than any of those omissions was my tendency to hide more and more, as my monomania increased its demands and encroached on my ability to act creatively, to explore life's potential. There have been times when my access to people was limited to the telephone, because I could not bring myself to leave the house; I just couldn't escape from the mirror long enough. That is why part of the value of Obsessive Compulsive Anonymous was that the meetings forced me out of hiding at least once a week.

Because OCA is modeled on AA, at the start of each meeting we would introduce ourselves by saying, "Hi, I'm…, and I have OCD." I found this ritual helpful, because I had for so long been in denial about my Disorder. When I began to attend the OCA meetings, I expected to find out how to cure myself and was dismayed to find that there were no cures for Obsessive/Compulsive Disorder. Consequently, very few people are completely and permanently liberated from its clutches. (In fact, I haven't met even one.) Initially, I found this knowledge disconcerting. On reflection, I had to admit that my Disorder was so time-consuming and disruptive, that *any* improvement was worth an effort. So I "kept coming back," even though repeating this slogan, ritualistically, at the close of each meeting made me cringe. And in spite of my reservations about the AA format, I found that listening to people tell their stories at the meetings gave me a great deal of insight both about the nature of my Disorder, and how to cope with it.

For me, a prerequisite for trying to ameliorate my Disorder was acknowledging my regret for all of the time lost to it. So I was especially encouraged when I listened to the older people in the group, people who had suffered with it even longer than I, express their determination to prevent their Obsessions and Compulsions from controlling the rest of their lives.

Pearl, whom I judged to be in her late sixties, had retired two years earlier. Her retirement had nearly coincided with the death of her mother, with whom she had always lived. So she had to face the loss of most of her basic emotional support system all at once, and at a relatively advanced age. What I admired about her was that instead of caving in to either depression or anxiety, she had made use of her free time to seek treatment and to involve herself in other activities which she found more or less satisfying, and which prevented her from getting stuck in incessant security checking. Unfortunately, her OCD could take another form: She went through agony making decisions about spending money. Through therapy, she had become aware that it was necessary to make decisions and move on. But even when she had wasted hours in indecisiveness, she would take heart from the realization that since her mother's death, she had, in fact, moved to another apartment and had even purchased new furniture for it. Then, she would again become absorbed in her Obsessions and express insecurities and doubts about choices that had already been made. In other words, Pearl would discuss her Obsessions and Compulsions objectively, and then, without a break, would begin acting them out, a phenomenon which was certainly not unique to her. Obsessive/Compulsive Disorder is incredibly pervasive and insidious, which is why it is virtually incurable. So therapists and sufferers both talk about reduction of symptoms.

At the time that I began going to OCA meetings, I had allowed the hair on top of my head to grow quite long. However, I continued to cut the sides and back daily, as close to the scalp as possible. I also continued to check for lashes that "needed" to be cut because they were the wrong texture or were growing in the wrong direction. And I'd developed a new depilatory variation: singling out long hairs on top of my head, because they were the 'wrong' length, the 'wrong' texture or made other hair fall the 'wrong' way; these I would break off, using the fingers of both hands. The scary thing about this variation was that, unlike all previous manifestations of the Disorder, I was doing this one in public, walking down the street, sitting on a bus, even sitting at an OCA meeting. I felt humiliated when a stranger commented on my breaking hairs as I walked down the street, but I couldn't stop.

Cognitive/Behavioral Therapy

In accordance with the 12-step philosophy, one was not supposed to discuss "outside treatments" during a meeting. I found this restriction to be counterproductive, since outside treatments may be an extremely important factor in coping with Obsessive/Compulsive Disorder. Fortunately, after the official meeting had concluded, it was possible to get information about different therapies and who was providing them. I soon learned that the two mainstays of treatment for OCD were antidepressants of a type called 'Selective Serotonin Re-uptake Inhibitors' and Cognitive/Behavioral Therapy. I wanted to avoid taking drugs, if possible, but I was both curious and hopeful about the possibilities of Cognitive/Behavioral Therapy.

I remembered the concept of Behavior Modification from an Experimental Psychology course I'd taken at Columbia years before. We read about Pavlov, who'd caused dogs to salivate at the sound of a bell, because the sound of the bell had been paired with food repetitively. His experiments teach us a great deal about certain kinds of learning in all mammals, including humans.

We also read Skinner's <u>Walden Two</u>, which reminded me of Huxley's dystopia, <u>Brave New World</u>, with its goal of an efficiently run society, in which everyone conforms. The thing is, if you're going to use Behavior Modification on people, it's got to be chosen by them—otherwise, it's Fascism. In that sense, Skinner had an ethical blind spot that initially turned public opinion against Behavior Modification techniques, which are potentially valuable tools for increasing human happiness. It turns out that Behavior Modification techniques can be useful in dealing with Anxiety Disorders, like Obsessive/Compulsive

Disorder, which have a strong biochemical component, whereas insight-oriented therapies promoting analysis and understanding are basically useless in treating such Disorders. For example, there are many people who have obsessive and controlling fears of contamination, which can be so extreme that the person is unable to leave the house, unable to function. One technique used by behaviorists to deal with such fears is "flooding," having the client touch a dirty object, like the bottom of a shoe, and then refrain from washing his hands for a gradually extended period of time. Eventually the client's fears may be worn down by this process, whereas understanding that he got this fear from a mother who was afraid of germs may be interesting, but probably won't alleviate the symptoms.

But why *Cognitive*/Behavioral? What is Cognitive Therapy? Its early practitioners had begun as insight-oriented therapists, psychoanalysts, looking for a more direct and reliable route to alleviating suffering than (for example) psychoanalysis. Cognitive Therapy differs from traditional psychoanalysis in that the therapist is concerned only with the conscious mind. Cognitive Therapy is based on the belief that our mental anguish is caused by cognitive error, not emotional illness. In other words, the therapist's job is to correct the client's irrational (self-destructive) beliefs.

One day my friend Lorna suggested that we go to see the "Albert Ellis show" that night. A well-known Cognitive Therapist, Ellis invented something called "Rational/Emotive" Therapy, which is a form of Cognitive Therapy . Ellis stated that most of our miseries are caused by "awfulizing" and "misattribution." "Awfulizing" means thinking things are worse than they really are. "Misattribution" usually involves taking responsibility (and feeling guilt) for things that aren't our fault. That night's show really was a performance. Ellis stood on a stage and called for volunteers to be therapized. I volunteered. Once I was on the stage, I felt like someone who's been chosen from the audience to help a magician do a trick. He asked me to present my problem. I told him that I had a son, in his mid-twenties, whom I loved dearly, who would do nothing but scream at me, hurling accusations at me for things that had happened twenty years before. No amount of apologies seemed to be enough. I was at my wits' end. Ellis said I should stop accepting blame. It was obvious to him that my son had a biochemical imbalance. Also, no matter what had happened in the past, I should insist that my son treat me in a respectful, civil manner. Ellis repeated pretty much what he had said, over and over, at each outrage of my son's that I mentioned. Ellis's repeated refrain, that I should stop allowing myself to be verbally abused, and insist on respectful treatment was amusing and easy to ridicule (he did basically the same thing with all of the volunteers). But the combination of Ellis's loud and insistent repetitions and the audience participation (people cheered him on) was a cathartic experience for me, much more powerful than sitting in a therapist's office conversing in dulcet tones would have been.

The Institute Of Behavior Therapy

After the Obsessive/Compulsive Anonymous meetings, I usually walked Pearl to the bus stop, and waited till the bus arrived, because she had some trepidation about being alone in an unfamiliar part of the city at night. She told me she was seeing a therapist named Steve Phillipson at the *Institute of Behavior Therapy*. She felt that he was helping her to understand and cope with her symptoms. It was true. She *had* become less anxious.

Several months passed before I went for therapy. I chose the *Institute of Behavior Therapy*, because of Pearl's recommendation, and also because it was affordable and conveniently located.

I had initially diagnosed myself, first to Steve Phillipson and then to David Miller, the therapist I was assigned to, as having Trichotillomania. My Trichotillomania was atypical, because I had always used tools–tweezers or scissors–rather than unaided fingers in my Depilatory Compulsion. But there was something else, another aspect of my Disorder, which I began to understand through therapy and reading. To begin with, I had read that Trichotillomania differs from Obsessive/Compulsive Disorder, in that it involves a Compulsion but no Obsession: OCD Compulsions are performed in order to ward off a danger like "don't step on a crack, or you'll break your mother's back"—endlessly. In my case, the hair cutting assuaged a visual Obsession. I began to think I had what is termed "Body Dysmorphic Disorder," which in about 50% of cases revolves around some aspect of face or hair. Dysmorphia means ugliness, and the Disorder is about fear of ugliness, which usually requires constant mirror checking. This Disorder was once called "Beauty Hypochondria." In my case, I was creating the ugliness I feared, but I never thought of that while I was involved in the Compulsion. On the contrary, I thought I was going to finally succeed in fixing the ugliness, once and for all. At the time I began therapy, I had consistently failed for 38 years to fix it once and for all. One definition of insanity is to be absolutely convinced that what has been tried many times and always failed is now going to work. So was I insane? Yes, when I was caught up in the Obsessive/Compulsive cycle. At other times, not.

It took time to make the connection between the Obsession and the Compulsion, so it was not possible initially for my therapist to devise meaningful Behavior Modification exercises for me. The exercises that are frequently successful in cases of Trichotillomania didn't somehow make sense to me. That's because they are designed to assuage a tactile need, like a scratching board for a cat. And unlike most people with Trichotillomania, I'm not exceptionally tactile. That is: I have the kind of sensation in my scalp, more subtle than an itch but even more compelling, that many people with Trichotillomania have; but I don't have the urge to touch objects, to feel textures, that most Trichotillomaniacs seem to have. I frequently rearrange objects Compulsively, not because of the way the textures feel, but rather because something in the visual aesthetic is disturbing me. (Apartment Dysmorphic Disorder?) Besides, there are many things I enjoy doing with my hands, when I'm able to stop cutting hair long enough to do them. I like to organize and rearrange and make art and sew. I can't be bothered wasting my time squeezing balls as Captain Queeg did in *The Caine Mutiny* (one of the exercises commonly used in treating hair pullers). Once I understood the Obsessional (visual) basis of my Compulsion to cut, I was able to devise my own Behavior Modification Techniques, which were usually successful for a while, things like covering mirrors and throwing my scissors away.

I remained in therapy with David Miller for three years, for two reasons. My relationship with my younger son was still bothering me, although the level of civility had improved to some extent since my session with Albert Ellis, but I still wanted guidance on how to proceed. Basically, whatever I said, my son Alex would reiterate a litany of memories which proved that I had been an awful mother to him. What I needed to communicate, in a way that he would accept, was that his being stuck in that mind-set prevented me from giving him the caring and affirmation he really wanted from me. Because David was of Alex's generation and shared much of his outlook on life, even certain personality traits, he could see things through a perspective which was similar to Alex's and was, therefore, able to help me to deflect Alex's accusations, rather than feeding into them, and to proceed from there.

Another way in which my weekly, and then biweekly, sessions with David helped was that he pressed me to focus on my Disorder during at least part of each session; it was always the last thing I wanted to think about. It was easy not to think about it, because I had allowed the hair on top of my head to grow quite long by the time I began therapy. The hair on the sides and back of my head was clipped short, but not bald. I had stopped cutting my lashes for a few weeks, so my right lid was no longer perpetually inflamed. I still checked both my hair and my lashes frequently, and there was the new Compulsion that had taken the place of the cutting: breaking individual long hairs on the top of my head. I was enjoying the look and feel of my long, wild top mop, and the short, stiff, almost continuous rows of lashes. It was summer, the first summer in 37 years that I was able to swim unconcerned about getting water in my right eye, "ruining" the lashes. I was euphoric.

Relapse

In August I went to Southern California to visit with my friend Maryanne. During the course of the week, I seemed to lose my center. I became emotionally dependent on Maryanne, who seemed to be always on the phone. I began to cut my hair. The Compulsion worked its way back surreptitiously: a cut here, two cuts there. I thought I could end it by having my hair cut professionally: "evened out", as I thought of it. Of course, it didn't work. The problem was in my perception. I had begun to see wrong hairs again, when I stood close to the mirror, which I was compelled to do. From the middle distance I could see that the hair still looked "normal" to a normal person, that is: someone other than me. I didn't "ruin" it, in that sense, until after I returned to my womb-like apartment in the East Village.

I had an appointment with David on the day I returned from California. I was wound up from not having slept for over 24 hours. My mind was racing, while my body didn't want to budge. I became possessed. That is, I had the sensation of watching myself go through a series of actions, which I saw clearly while I did them, were self-destructive. But the self who knew and wanted to prevent what was about to occur was paralyzed. The logic of my situation forced the realization that it was essential that I keep my appointment with David, if only for the sake of getting out of the house. With horrified fascination, I heard my self-destruct demon call David and cancel the appointment, citing exhaustion as an excuse. Oh sure. At one point I thought, "My hair looks OK now; but if I make one more cut, I'll end up ruining it." And I did.

By October I was cutting the lashes as close to the lid as possible. And because I had stopped cutting for about a month, thinking I was making progress, I was full of disappointment and self-loathing. And since I'd become accustomed to being all right with my appearance, I was more intolerant of my present unattractiveness. I spent the next six months dealing with wigs and false eyelashes. I hated the way they felt, but my need to have what I considered an acceptable appearance outweighed the physical discomfort. I felt more hopeless than ever, and continued weekly therapy sessions, mostly as an outlet for frustration. But I was too embarrassed by the visibility of my relapse to go back to the Obsessive/Compulsive Anonymous group.

Diary Selections 1992

Shortly after I began therapy with David Miller, he suggested that I keep a diary of what was going on with my Disorder: what I did and how I felt. The following are excerpts from it:

T.R.I.C.H.O.T.I.L.L.O.M.A.N.I.A.... It's eating up my time, my life, rushing in to fill every gap...

10/13/92   2am—There were so many things I could have done today and this evening. And all I did was groom: bathe, brush my teeth, smooth Retin-A on my face. And, as so frequently happens, I got stuck in my Compulsion to repeatedly check and cut my hair, hour after hour. I did not do what I'd planned, which was to play with my new computer. Now I'm exhausted, ready for sleep. But before allowing myself to nod out, I'm going to trace exactly what occurred:

Once having decided to work with the computer, I perceived two options: attach the printer and see if I could get it going, or go over the commands in the Macintosh Start Up Booklet. I can see now that the latter choice would have been better. But at the time, each possibility attracted and repelled me with equivalent force, and I allowed myself, once more, to cave in to the frustration of not being able to make a choice. Frustration, and then, as the hours went by, and I still hadn't accomplished anything, guilt. So I punished myself with mirror/scissors torture, and was punished afterwards by suffering baldness and lashlessness, and was angry at myself for having caused the condition. And on it went. But there is something else, something I can't control,

18

a compelling urge which crops up even in the midst of joy. Or perhaps it erupts then, because I feel I don't deserve euphoria. So the checking and cutting can be precipitated by mild frustration, guilt, or anything that provokes anxiety. The end result is almost always self-loathing. And in the middle, there is a hiccup of the mind, a primitive grooming response gone berserk.

10/14/92   2:30am   It's been 24 hours since I cut my hair. I'm aware of a slight, but constant, and therefore annoying ache caused by an implant in my upper left gum. One function of a Compulsion is to distract the mind from pain, either physical or psychic. If I don't indulge in this drugless sedation, I'll be forced to deal with my dental dilemma.

One obvious way to avoid cutting is to be away from home. This is not an absolute. I remember this past summer, breaking long top-hairs, one by one, while walking to the East River Park. For the past two weeks, I've prevented myself from touching, much less tearing, my hair when I'm outside by wearing a wig. I've tried wearing the wig at home too, and what happens is that I began to cut the wig, concentrating on the right side, just as I do my hair. So, to return to strategy, I stayed out of the house this evening, First, I visited my aunt in the hospital, then I had a long late dinner with a friend. So wearing a wig and staying out do curtail my Compulsions, but not satisfactorily. That is, I still have a guilty sense of having procrastinated with respect to doing what I need to do, namely, getting started with the computer.

10/15/92   2:30am   I just spent an hour cutting the hair on the right side by touch-kinetic torture (no mirror, except for the one in my mind). It was a section I'd planned to cut in a week. But as usual, I couldn't live with the 'imperfection.' Thinking "It will have to be cut" translates to "cut it now." I feel powerless. None of the plans, injunctions, conditions, bribes, or bargains I've given myself, in an effort to quit checking and cutting, has ever worked. When I stopped or slowed down, not only was I unaware that I was no longer spending most of my waking hours on my Obsessions and Compulsions, I wasn't even conscious of the improvement, until the Disorder had again insidiously crept up on me. On one occasion, I did realize that I hadn't cut in over a month and wasn't checking in the mirror every few minutes. This was followed by a moment of exultation, followed by fear, the realization that "it" could start at any time, without even consulting me.

10/16/92   10:30am   I missed work today. Disaster. Now the Disorder has gone beyond eating up my free time. It's threatening my livelihood as well. I'm filled with self-disgust, as well as fear of losing my job. It used to be like this a lot, 10, 20, 30 years ago. But it hadn't happened recently, so it's a jolt.

I can see from skimming this diary that, whether or not I cut my hair, I feel that it's out of my control. I feel helpless, but not defeated. Fortunately, my Disorder is a currently popular one, so there's plenty of experimentation, some of which may be helpful to me.

Showcase For Therapists

In December, a woman named Stacey, whom I had met at O/CA meetings, called. She was drumming up business for a group that she had just initiated, which met on Tuesday night. Her group was not a 12-step group, which predisposed me in its favor. It was actually more of a lecture series than a support group, with professional speakers who would lecture on some aspect of Obsessive/Compulsive Disorder or an Obsessive/Compulsive Spectrum Disorder, and then be available for questions. The fee was an affordable $8. Stacey's lecture series functioned as a showcase for therapists performing for an audience of potential clients, which was why several of the most prominent therapists in the field were willing to donate the time and effort to make a presentation there.

The folding chairs were packed with an eagerly anticipatory audience. The speaker that evening was Ari Kiev, Medical Director of the Social Psychiatry Research Institute. His perspective was informed by the practice of Zen Buddhism. He invited us to view our Obsessions and Compulsions as simply another aspect of life, rather than something split off and separate. His words made me acutely aware of my tendency to think of the time I spent cutting my hair and lashes, minutely examining facial flaws, or placing and replacing objects around my apartment for hours on end as "unofficial" time, unrecognized time. There was something about Dr. Kiev, a receptivity, which encouraged people to be forthcoming about the pain they suffered. He called on a slim blond woman with regular features, who reminded me of myself at a younger age. I almost couldn't believe what I was hearing.

"I pulled our my eyelashes for 24 years," she said. "It always made me feel incredibly ugly. But I couldn't stop, until I began taking Anafranil six weeks ago."

I had finally encountered someone who did what I had done for so many years. "It made me feel incredibly ugly." Yes!

Dr. Kiev's wife was there. They were opposites. He was plump, and gentle, with rounded edges. She was sharp, emaciated, and abrupt, with enormous darting black eyes. She radiated a crackling intensity. During the question and answer period, a man spoke about having to check his mailbox several times after he got home, never quite trusting that he hadn't missed something. Ari Kiev's wife shot up out of her chair, pointed a long, bony finger at the speaker, and demanded that he promise her that he wouldn't check his mailbox more than once that night. It was as if she were trying to mesmerize him into relinquishing his Disorder. I wondered if such shock tactics would work. Since OCD is like a "hiccup of the mind"—to quote Judith Rappoport, I suspected that the (temporary) cure, as with hiccups, is whatever a person is doing or having done to them when it stops.

Stacey's series provided a good opportunity to become aware of the way the professionals perceived Obsessive/Compulsive Disorder, and the Spectrum of related Disorders, and what they considered the best methods of treatment. The therapists could be divided into two categories: behavioral therapists, who were mostly psychologists, and psycho pharmacologists, who were psychiatrists. There were also a few, both Ph.D.s and M.D.s, who gave relatively equal weight to Drug and Behavior Therapy. The Ph.D.s, of course, had to refer their clients to the psychiatrists for meds. And there was an occasional mention of Cognitive Therapy, particularly for cases of Pure Obsession. I learned that at clinics which treat Anxiety Disorders, (which include Obsessive/Compulsive Disorder and the many Obsessive/Compulsive Spectrum Disorders), behavior therapists and psycho pharmacologists often work as a team. This is particularly true of hospitals, which offer inpatient therapy.

One of the speakers at the lecture series was Ken Garfunkle, a Behaviorist, who was part of such a team at the Anxiety Disorders Clinic of Columbia Presbyterian Medical Center. There was something about both the narrowness and the intensity of his focus, which reminded me of the Disorder itself, as I experience it. He seemed to have an instinctive understanding of its nature. And I was excited by his expectation of achieving results in a few weeks to a few months. I inquired about his fees, which turned out to be out of my range; I did not have medical coverage. However, Dr. Garfunkle said that there was a study being done at Columbia Presbyterian, which was free to participants. The study was an attempt to estimate the relative effectiveness of Behavior Therapy alone, drug therapy alone, or a combination of the two. He said that all who participated in the study would eventually have access to both kinds of therapy, gratis.

Another speaker whom I encountered at Stacey's series was Dr. Ulla Kristina Laakso. Dr. Laakso was lovely to look at, glamorous, with exquisite pale coloring set off by a wonderfully tailored dress and jacket suit in gunmetal with a silky sheen. She was Finnish, and her accent reminded me of the lilting accents I'd heard in Sweden. Dr. Laakso compared treatment methods in Europe and the United Sates. She felt that the Europeans had been there first with what worked, eulogizing Anafranil, which she said was the first drug used successfully to treat Obsessive/Compulsive Disorder. Dr. Laakso said that once the drug was publicized, the number of people who came forward to be treated was much greater than anyone anticipated. She reminded those of us who had sought relief from our Disorder from therapists lacking specialized knowledge about OCD and its treatment, of the frustration and despair we had experienced, when the therapy failed, as we now know, it is likely to. Dr. Laakso's anecdotes about people who were suddenly and completely submerged in OCD and then, just as suddenly, recovered after being treated with Anafranil, were as dramatic as her appearance. She stressed that correct diagnosis was important in order to find the right quantity of the right drug or combination of drugs, adding that fine tuning of drugs by an expert psycho pharmacologist like herself could make all the difference.

I learned a great deal about the subtle twists and turns of the Obsessive/Compulsive mind, my own and others', from the presentations of the therapists and, even more, from the questions of an audience thirsty for information and the therapists' answers to those questions. Of course, the quest for more and more information is frequently one of the characteristics of the Disorder. A common feature of OCD is the feeling that if you only had this one vital piece of the puzzle, all of the others would fall into place. Another central factor in OCD is doubt. And my own doubts–about whether I was going about treating my Disorder in the "right" way–were exacerbated by the various presentations that I listened to. I was aware that the therapists who spoke were angling for clients or research subjects for themselves or the institutions they were affiliated with. And I was always sold. I would think, "Am I seeing the right therapist? I can't afford a 'top flight' therapist. Maybe I should go into the 'free-treatment-as-a-research-subject' program at Columbia Presbyterian. But it's too far from where I live, and besides, if I can't stand the drug and have to drop out, it will all have been for naught."

Dr. Laakso,
Psychophamacologist

When I decided to try medication to combat my Disorder, I went to Dr. Laakso. I came to think of her as a human cash register, but her greed and my need seemed to coincide. Dr. Laakso charged $50 for a 15-minute session. Who ever heard of a 15-minute session? But I thought, how long does it take to write a prescription? Actually, Dr. Laakso spent most of the 15 minutes telling me I should get SSI, a type of Federal Disability Insurance that comes with Medicaid. At the time, I was teaching in the City's Department of Adult Education, which I wasn't about to give up in order to go on the dole to get medical insurance. The SSI allowance just isn't big enough to live on.

The first antidepressant that Dr. Laakso put me on was a sample of Anafranil (clomipramine). Anafranil is a Tricyclic, not an SSRI (Selective Serotonin Re-Uptake Inhibitor), which is the type of antidepressant usually recommended for Obsessive/Compulsive Disorder and Obsessive/Compulsive Spectrum Disorders. In Europe, Anafranil had been used with some success in the treatment of OCD. But the SSRIs have proven to be at least as effective, and safer. In any case, I stopped taking Anafranil on the second day, because my mouth became so extremely dry that I had a panic attack, which is unusual for me. Then Dr. Laakso prescribed Prozac (fluoxetine), the first of the SSRIs. I had used Prozac once before, and it ended my one bout of severe depression, which had lasted for several months. One 20-milligram pill seemed to turn a switch in my brain, completely eliminating the depression. I stopped taking the drug after two months, and did not revert to depression. I told Dr. Laakso that although Prozac had worked wonderfully well for my depression, it did nothing to alleviate my anxiety. To the contrary! The depression had all but eliminated my checking and cutting, because, in a depressed state, I didn't care about anything, even my appearance. But when the depression was gone, my checking and cutting had returned. Dr. Laakso said she wasn't surprised that the 20-milligram pill, which was effective for depression, didn't affect anxiety. She said that OCD patients took 60 and 80 milligrams of Prozac daily. Although I began gradually, it was difficult for me to tolerate 60 milligrams a day of Prozac. Making me feel nerved up, intense, with palpitations and sweaty palms. It was almost like Dexedrine but without the positive effect of concentrating the mind, which was what had made Dexedrine so popular when I was in college. Still, in spite of my discomfort with the high dosage of Prozac, I was willing to give it a try. I hoped fervently that it, that something, would make a serious dent in my symptoms. The following diary entries were made while I was taking 60 milligrams a day of Prozac.

Diary Selections 1993

8/2/93   Tonight, for the first time in ages, I didn't either cut or break my hair. I did check in the mirror from time to time, but the checking was frustrating, when it didn't culminate in some form of hair removal. So checking episodes were frequent, but short. There was one form of the Disorder that I became immersed in: checking with my fingers, to see if any hairs "needed" to be cut. Once I became conscious of what I was doing, I switched to rubbing my head, for as much as 10 minutes at a time. It was a calming, reassuring alternative to my usual self-torture, and an antidote to the underlying anxiety. Perhaps the switch from cutting and breaking hair to rubbing my head is the result of having taken 60 milligrams of Prozac a day for the past two weeks. Still, I can see why all of the people writing in the field say that the best treatment is SSRIs and Behavior Modification Therapy in tandem. Ameliorating the Disorder requires conscious intent, even if chemical aid is used. There is a tendency for the body to become tolerant of any psycho tropic drug, which then becomes less and less effective, which makes relapse more than likely. So if you haven't learned techniques for coping with the Disorder by the time the effectiveness of the drug begins to wear off, you're likely to be so full of self-loathing that you let yourself slide right back into full-time out-of-control, *in spite of the drug.*

8/3/93   Today was my first session with David Miller, since the Prozac has (apparently) kicked in. And, probably because of the drug, I was finally able to think about behavior modification techniques. I told

David that the Prozac seemed to be working, and my desire to cut had so diminished that it required no great effort to resist.

"However," I said, "I still find myself checking in the mirror for no reason other than to torture myself. This week, I'm going to get a handle on it. I'll only allow myself to check before I leave the house."

Looking in the mirror is, for the Body Dysmorphic, what eating is to the person with Binge Eating Disorder. It's almost impossible to limit what, for most people, is a normal activity. I told David that my mirror checking wasn't limited to home, that I did it, more or less surreptitiously, in the windows and mirrors I passed as I walked around the City. David thought I should resolve to cut that out too. To me, it seemed improbable that I'd be able to resist looking at my reflection in mirrors I passed on the street. My shadow on the sidewalk was another source of information about the shape of my hair.

I told David that although my Disorder certainly hadn't vanished, it seemed more manageable than it ever had before.

"But there's a down side to my new freedom," I said. "I'm experiencing feelings I've never allowed myself to experience before, like sadness, regrets about the past, misgivings about the future. A Disorder like mine makes you emotionally independent; you're so enmeshed in its constant demands, there isn't much room for other concerns.

8/12/93   I went for a whole week without either cutting or excessive checking, either in the mirror or manually. Then, I slipped. And once having begun, couldn't prevent myself from continuing to cut—for six hours. Fortunately, amazingly, the Compulsion had run its course by the following evening.

Four days later, I visited friends at their house in upstate New York. It was an event, a celebration of their 10th anniversary, their new home, love and nature. There was a massive array of tempting food, and I allowed myself to overindulge. Having just lost six pounds, I was furious at myself for putting half of it back on in one fell swoop. My hair cutting on this occasion may have been a punishment for having over-indulged in food to the point of nausea. I punished myself for loss of self-control by inflicting more loss of self-control on myself. That way, I could feel really powerless. Having obliterated whatever little faith I might have retained, what hope was there that I'd be able to accomplish anything I set out to do? Instead, I could wallow in the agony of having thwarted myself once again.

8/13/93   I've given up on Prozac. I don't know if I experienced a placebo effect during those first two euphoric weeks, or if my brain responded to it immediately, and then learned to tolerate it, also quickly. In any case, I didn't see any appreciable gains after that. Dr. Laakso wanted me to keep upping my dosage. At 60 milligrams a day I was still checking and cutting like crazy and had an unpleasantly edgy feeling, which I hadn't had before. Perhaps that article in the *Times* was right. Maybe I can Cognitive/Behavioral my neurons into letting the serotonin hang out in the synapses, like it's supposed to.

8/14/93   My mother is an isolator. I could have learned to isolate from her, but I believe that it's an inherited tendency. Like my mother, I resent being pulled out of my own head and forced to focus on another person, another person's thought. Unlike my mother, I feel guilty about my reluctance to listen to people. I think this difference is the result of different expectations of women in our respective generations. For me, the craving to remain in my own head has been in constant conflict with the demands of my life.

This week's relapse, like the one last August, was provoked by staying with other people, which made me insecure about being able to fulfill my need to isolate. The onset of my Disorder also occurred in an environment where I was not assured of privacy: summer camp. It's the potential for incursions on my privacy, rather than simply being away from home, that provokes the Disorder. When I've traveled alone—in Mexico, Greece, India—the mirror checking and attendant Compulsions subsided.

10/1/1993   Damn! I've lost another night to cutting and rearranging hair, and moving lashes around with tweezers. Both my hair and my lashes seem all right now; but it's 4 am, and I have to wake up in three hours.

Before I had any knowledge about my Disorder, I didn't regret the time I'd spent on it after I was released, momentarily, and could move away from the mirror and live my life. I was just grateful for the respite. It is only since I've become aware of the nature of the Disorder that I have been bitter about the aggregate time spent on it and, at the same time, feel guilty about current episodes. I'm no longer innocent, and therefore not responsible. I feel that I should be able to flush out and annihilate that treacherous part of my brain which continues to be seduced into surrendering to endless Obsession and Compulsion.

11/15/1993   I've been overtaken by creeping paralysis of will this week. The most worrisome result is having been quite late to work every day. Other evidence of my intentions being blocked was that it took me three days to sew three buttons on a blazer and five days to make planned calls. Staring at the blockage precipitates a cutting episode, which then perpetuates itself, even after the miasma has blown away, buttons sewn, calls made, and back to work more-or-less on time.

12/1/93   Checking, and—what a surprise!—finding something wrong; and then, taking steps to "correct" it, which could last for hours. I finally escape to some other pursuit, only to be sucked back into the mirror again for another bout. It's a stalling technique, a defense against living, against being inundated by changing reality. It's always in the interstices of my life, sometimes becoming so pervasive, I'm stuck, unable to perform any other activity. I'm drawn back to a magnetized mirror by the thrilling probability that I will again be tortured by the horrific effects of light and shadow as perceived through my retina, mesmerized by that perception, attempting frantically, endlessly, to fix it, usually making my lashes/hair objectively worse. On rare occasions, I'm able to make the hairs more symmetrical—for five minutes or a day. One of the most upsetting aspects of this Disorder is the anxiety created by not being able to count on myself, which in turn fills me with resentment of others who are in some way counting on me, and guilt for not having been able to do what I thought I should do, even though I can't do it.

Group Therapy

Soon after I first attended Stacey's lecture series, I began Steve Phillipson's Friday evening group therapy sessions. When I first came to the Institute of Behavior Therapy, I had been interviewed by Dr. Phillipson. My first impression of him was that he was an attractive young man who was rather stuck on himself. My second impression was that my first impression wasn't wrong, but that spending a couple of hours every other week with someone who was enjoying being himself, living his life, was not a bad thing. Also, I found that Dr. Phillipson was attentive to what his patients were saying and to the implications of what they were saying. He was good at catching OCD thought patterns and exposing them, in a manner which respected the individual whose self-defeating thought pattern was being examined. Dr. Phillipson fully employed the cognitive aspect of Cognitive/Behavioral Therapy.

There are major differences between a self-help support group and a therapist-led group. In the former, it is essential that each member feel that he or she is respected by all of the other members, thus establishing trust, an emotionally secure framework within which people can discuss things which are painful, embarrassing, or otherwise disturbing. For many, this secure framework needs to be based on rules of engagement, which are spelled out and anticipate most contingencies. It is this framework which enables the 12-step "fellowships" based on Alcoholics Anonymous to continue to proliferate. In contrast, in a therapist-led group, it is only necessary that all of the participants trust the therapist. It is the therapist who provides the emotionally secure framework. And because the therapist assumes the responsibility of being a just arbiter, the patients/clients need not be responsible for censoring either themselves or each other. Nor do they have to monitor the tendency to "do" their obsessive thinking, as one is expected to do in Obsessive/Compulsive Anonymous. The therapist can be relied upon as a reality check, making the patient aware of being caught up in an obsessive knot, and also validating perceptive, constructive contributions with regard either to one's own situation or another's. The last was hard to get used to.

I had been schooled in O/CA not to "take other people's inventory." Here, the format was that after each person spoke about what was going on with them, especially with regard to how they were coping (or not) with their Obsessive/Compulsive symptoms, every other member of the group was invited, in turn, to share his or her observations and recommendations. Then Dr. Phillipson had the final word: synthesis, criticism, whatever was called for, and then, on to the next case.

During my first session, a woman named Lee shocked me by saying something which would have drawn a severe reprimand at any of the self help groups I've ever participated in. After I'd given a brief rundown of my symptoms, she told me my Disorder was so severe that I should be hospitalized. I gasped, astonished as well as outraged. Dr. Phillipson simply told her that hospitalization wasn't the answer for everyone. Later in the session, I learned that in addition to having a form of Obsessive/Compulsive Spectrum Disorder similar to mine, Lee had Bi-Polar Disorder and because of it, had been institutionalized for much of her adult life. (She and I were contemporaries.) This put her "advice" to me in a different light, for two reasons. First, she was projecting her own experience. Hospitalization, although she loathed it, was for Lee not unthinkable. The second reason for her apparent lack of consideration for my feelings, I believe, is that people are infantilized in institutions. And Lee's maturation during the few years since her release hadn't been helped by living with her mother in the same relationship as before: rebellious adolescent daughter/domineering mother. So, although I found Lee hard to take, I sympathized with her. I also admired her, because she was not allowing resentment for the lost years to sabotage her efforts to lead a full, satisfying life in the present.

Naturally, people with more severe and intractable Disorders remain in therapist-led groups longer. Most of the people in Dr. Phillipson's group had been coming for years and were very attached to Dr. Phillipson, whom they looked to for support and comfort as well as for a reality check. One woman, Ramona, said that Dr. Phillipson was like a father/mother/husband/brother all rolled into one. She had been his patient for seven years.

Another long-term participant was Ralph, whose Disorder was so pervasive that, at 50, he continued to live with his parents, although he recognized that his parents' attitude toward him was enabling, not empowering. His complaints about his parents were frequently followed by excuses for them. He despaired of ever being able to live on his own. Ralph had had a brief, successful college career, until his symptoms became so pronounced that they subsumed most of his mental activity and he was unable either to continue his studies or to function independently, even in the relatively relaxed environment of a university. At the time I encountered him, his anxiety was so all-encompassing that he was incapable of completing a thought. He would become so distracted by something (anxiety provoking) that he noticed along the way, that he would forget the thought's original destination. I knew that he was taking medication. (I was the only one in the group who wasn't.) But whatever the medication was, it didn't seem to help him to gather and order his scattered thoughts. I didn't know if there was any brand of therapy, verbal or pharmacological, which could help him to become significantly more functional. But participating in Dr. Phillipson's group enhanced his life because the support and acceptance he received both from Dr. Phillipson and from other members of the group was an antidote to his parents' disparaging attitude toward him.

Mark's Obsessional thinking mostly revolved around mistakes he'd made on his editing job. He said he would rework the same minuscule error over and over, sometimes for weeks, until he'd made another one. He castigated himself for not having prevented the error before handing the work in and was in perpetual anxiety about being reprimanded by his supervisor either for his errors or for taking too long to do the work, which was unavoidable because of his extreme vigilance in his effort to prevent errors. Ultimately, of course, he was afraid of losing his job. Dr. Phillipson tried to help Mark to be less perfectionistic about his work, and to accept realistic uncertainty with respect to keeping his job, to admit the possibility of being fired without being consumed by it. The latter thought is a good example of Cognitive Therapy: admitting to the realization that what you fear may actually happen, without becoming riveted to the possibility and paralyzed by it.

Mark was in his late 30s and married, happily, since he and his wife enjoyed a mutually caring and supportive relationship. Mark listened attentively to others in the group and when Dr. Phillipson asked for his comment on another patient's presentation, his somewhat tentative remarks were frequently insightful.

Pete, the youngest member of the group, was in his early 20s. He, like Ralph, was incapable of living on his own. But when his parents retired to Florida, rather than moving with them and perpetuating his dependence on them, he had opted to remain in New York and live in a group home. His Obsessions revolved around the possible contamination of food that he was served at the home or, occasionally. in restaurants. The effects of his Disorder, dangerous weight loss and malnutrition were the same as those of anorexic patients, though the Obsessional basis was different. Pete had frequently needed to be hospitalized and fed through an IV, and he lived in fear of having to undergo another hospitalization. Clearly though, being hospitalized provided "secondary gains". When he was being kept alive by others, he was able to surrender his anxiety.

Pete was also seeing a psychiatrist, a condition of his living in the group home, which was all paid for by Medicaid. This psychiatrist prescribed an anti-psychotic medication, Pimozide (perphenazine), which can cause permanent Tardive Dyskinesia, a Disorder which involves major loss of control over voluntary movement and an increase in involuntary movement. There are other potentially serious side effects with Pimozide, which is why Dr. Phillipson did not approve of the medication for Pete. Why take such a serious risk, when there is neither psychosis or Tourette Syndrome syndrome, the two types of Disorder that Pimozide is recommended for? But Pete felt too incompetent to refuse the recommendation of this authority figure, the psychiatrist. I continued to hope that he would be able to substitute Steve's authority for the psychiatrist's.

We sometimes went out for a bite after the session. Once, I went with Ramona, Mark, and Pete. Both before and after the food was served, Pete went into gory detail about how the food and drink in the restaurant might be contaminated. Ramona had such a warm nurturing attitude toward Pete that he felt secure enough to consume all of his Danish and coffee, while continuing to express fears about it. I, on the other hand, became so nauseated through ingesting his words, that after the first three mouthfuls I was unable to continue.

More frequently after group sessions, some of us would hang out for a half an hour or so in the waiting room adjacent to the offices. This was possible because we were the last patients of the evening. Once, as we stood chatting in this anteroom, I mentioned to Ramona, whom I'd come to like, that I had attended what I assumed would be a support group but was actually a lecture series featuring psychiatrists and psychologists who specialized in anxiety Disorders. And, although it wasn't what I'd anticipated, I was enthusiastic about it and expected to attend the next installment. I mentioned that it had been organized by someone named Stacey.

Unexpectedly, Ramona's face darkened. She became enraged. Evidently, she and Stacey were more than slightly acquainted, and the relationship had ended badly, Ramona feeling victimized by Stacey. Ramona said that originally the two of them had planned to start the group together and that, after they'd both put a great deal of time and effort into the planning, Stacey had simply dumped her, without warning, and proceeded to organize the group herself. To this day, I don't know what the original source of friction was. But I do know that Ramona is passionate, empathetic, expressive, and articulate, and she can be both self-righteous and unrelenting. Stacey is a blunter instrument. Her orientation is practical. She is cool and secretive, though not unperceptive. I left Dr. Phillipson's group after four months, but I remained friends with Ramona for over a year. I enjoyed her perspective on life and her sympathetic understanding of other people's issues. But her self-righteousness, even if it was not directed at me, made me nuts, provoking me to scream at her. I was always sorry afterwards, realizing that I was driving her away. The last thing that happened between us was that Ramona was on her way to my house and called to say she was having a panic attack and needed to go home. I called later to see if Ramona was okay. She replied that her panic attack has subsided. I haven't heard from her since.

While I was in Dr. Phillipson's group, I began to consider the relationship between OCD (and OCSDs) and gainful employment. According to the statistics I'd read, a large percentage of OCD sufferers are unable to work for extended periods of time. Some of Dr. Phillipson's patients, like Ralph and Pete, were so enmeshed in their Disorder that they were unemployable. Lee worked in a "protected" work environment, where both her OCD and Bi-Polar Disorder were known and appropriate allowances made. Mark continued to struggle with the demands of an editing job, which his Disorder rendered excruciatingly problematic. And Fred was similarly anxious about being able to fulfill the requirements of his job, teaching in a vocational high school. Like Mark, he would become greatly exercised over every trivial error he made. In addition, he had an acute sense of shame, and felt humiliated in the eyes of his students, who, he assumed, expected perfection of him. He also feared that his principal or other members of the faculty would be so outraged by any misstatement or misspelling that he made, that even a single such error might result in his being fired. In expressing all of these insecurities, Fred made a compelling demand for reassurance, which Dr. Phillipson usually managed to avoid giving. Dr Phillipson approached work-related anxieties from two angles. The first was to distinguish reasonable diligence from unproductive perfectionism. The second was to induce us to accept the idea that losing one's job is a possibility for most people.

Ramona, who was not currently employed, suffered from a similar perfectionism, which I was witness to when she became stuck in the process of decision-making involved in purchasing three items in a grocery. When she was employed, she had become stymied, spending hours checking and rechecking work that she had completed, staying at the office till 1am and 2am. She quit, and was able to get disability insurance. The anxiety that Ramona suffered when she was employed certainly sounded like a nightmare. In that respect her response to the demands of a job was similar to that of Fred and Jim. In all three cases the anxiety was both intense and unremitting, and required a diligence so extreme that it threw them into a state of nervous exhaustion. But there's another factor to consider. Ramona loathed and resented her clerical job. In contrast, both the teacher and the editor got considerable satisfaction from their jobs, as well as a heavy load of anxiety. In other words, although OCD certainly can undermine one's ability to work, job satisfaction–in terms of both identification with purposes of the enterprise and enjoyment of process–is crucial in determining whether a person relinquishes a hold on employment, or frantically grasps onto it.

My own ability to maintain employment has been impacted by my Disorder in a somewhat different fashion. During the years following my discovery of the name and nature of my Disorder, I was teaching for the New York City Board of Education's Office of Adult and Continuing Education. Like Fred, I enjoyed teaching: presenting material, clarifying concepts, interacting with students. And the pay was decent. Yet I was continually putting my job in jeopardy by getting stuck checking and rechecking, "fixing" and "refixing" my hair and/or lashes, when I knew that doing so was going to make me late. In that respect, it was no different from what occurred prior to any event where I needed to show up. I hated my perpetual tardiness. My inability to break away from the mirror in order to keep appointments made me feel helpless and worthless. I had to approach each meeting with an apology and an excuse.

Trichotillomania Support Group

During this period, I was diagnosing myself (and being diagnosed by Dave and Steve) as having Trichotillomania. So I was interested when Stacey, always full of useful information, told me about a support group specifically for people with Trichotillomania. She gave me the number of the group's organizer, Vivian.

My first reaction to Vivian, on the phone, was negative. What a snob! She actually used the phrase "our sort of person," when speaking of admitting new members into the group. For me, the support group concept has to do with a common focus, problem, issue, which the participants put their heads together to try to understand, resolve, or ameliorate, or, at the very least, to offer the relief of knowing you're not the only one suffering in this way. Also, Vivian's voice was unpleasantly querulous, though there was no argument. Yet much of what she related to me made me feel I wanted to be in this group. Vivian had been on a summer retreat organized by a woman named Christina Dubowsky, whose name, I subsequently learned, is synonymous with the recovering Trichotillomaniac. Vivian had been exhilarated by the experience: three days during which the participants had a chance to listen to and question the most highly regarded professionals who treat Trichotillomania. Even more important, she'd been in contact with 200 other women, who shared the secret shame she'd been coping with for five decades–even longer than I.

There were four other women in the group, two in their late 20s, one in her early 30s, and one in her early 40s. I was 51, so every decade from twenties through sixties was represented in our tiny group. All of the participants were articulate and well informed, which I enjoyed and benefited from. What I disliked in this group of high-powered achievers was the pervasive–and infectious–high tension.

At one meeting, we watched a video that one of the women brought. It was of a therapist named Carol Novak, discussing and illustrating techniques which she said she'd used successfully to treat Trichotillomania. They all involved using one's hands in some way other than pulling out one's hair. When we discussed the video afterwards, the others, except for Carol, who wasn't interested in behavior therapy, felt that Ms. Novak's recommendations made sense. They'd had a frisson of recognition. For me, the techniques described in the video (like squeezing rubber balls repeatedly) didn't resonate. There are many things I enjoy doing with my hands, including nothing, if I can only get them out of my hair long enough to do them. I hoped I would discover behavior modification techniques that worked for me, but I knew these weren't suitable. So did I have Trichotillomania at all, or, did I simply have a form of Body Dysmorphic Disorder that revolved around hair? I decided that I did, indeed, have Tricotillomania, because, once I began breaking hairs or cutting without a mirror, I frequently had a tingling sensation in my scalp, which informed me of where the next hair(s) should be broken or cut.

I always felt something of an outsider in this group, partly because they were all hair pullers and I was a hair cutter and breaker, but more profoundly because they discounted the concept of OC Spectrum, feeling that they had little in common with OCD sufferers despite the fact that the same therapies–Specific Serotonin Re-uptake Inhibitors and Behavior Modification Therapy–have had appreciable success with large numbers of both OCD and Tricotillomania sufferers. These women were confident that if they could only kick the hair-pulling habit, they would be "normal". I felt that my Disorder might very possibly change form, because it had changed form in the past. Paradoxically, it was through participating in this Trichotillomania group that I began to recognize the variety of manifestations my Disorder had assumed, beginning in early childhood.

Carol thought that her hair pulling had begun because she had been sexually molested by her stepfather, and that the Disorder's persistence into the present was the result of her mother's continued denial of what had occurred. Carol was seeing a psychoanalyst twice a week, and, although she acknowledged that the treatment had not ameliorated her Trichotillomania, she felt that her sessions with this doctor, with whom she had a close rapport, were essential. She was also taking Prozac, which she said made her feel better, less depressed. But, as in my case after the first two weeks, the Prozac had not had any discernible impact on her hair pulling.

Among the members of the group, Carol's Disorder most resembled mine. For both of us, the most time-consuming and emotionally fraught and exhausting Compulsions revolved around the perpetual need to "correct" the flaws that we ourselves had created during the preceding segment of the Obsessive/Compulsive cycle. And, like Carol, I felt that the focus of an Obsessive/Compulsive or Obsessive/Compulsive Spectrum Disorder was related to what had happened in your life preceding the onset of the Disorder. Unlike Carol, I didn't at all discount the effects of brain chemistry as the other necessary, but not in itself sufficient, component of Tricotillomania, OCD, or any related Disorder.

Visualizations

One evening, I was at my friend Millie's house. I had discussed my Disorder with her and told her that although everyone said that a Cognitive/Behavioral approach was the only one that had proven successful in treating OC Spectrum Disorders, I felt that it would help me to have a better understanding of what had gone on in my childhood. The problem was that except for a few striking incidents which had become "family stories," my childhood, even my adolescence, was pretty much of a blur to me, in spite of having tried to penetrate it with psychotherapy and introspection. Millie gave me her copy of Bradshaw's *Healing The Shame That Binds,* which she said explained in detail a technique for accessing early memories. I looked forward both to reading the book and to putting the technique, called "inner child work," into practice. Then, after I'd completed the former, but not yet begun the latter, I spent an evening with another friend, Gloria. I told her about my desire to do inner child work, as Bradshaw recommends, by visualizing my inner child and being with her as my present adult self, but that I hadn't yet been able to get started, fascinated though I was by the experiences of Bradshaw's patients. Gloria thought it might help to have something representing my inner child to focus on. She gave me a miniature stuffed rabbit, which was perfect, since my sister once alluded to people with pale lashes and brows like mine as "rabbits."

So, armed with Bradshaw and the bunny, I set out to visualize and interact with a former self. At first I just visualized:

I saw myself at the age one. I was in the spacious foyer of our seven room apartment, walking uncertainly. My shoes held my feet and ankles firmly, which was uncomfortable. And the bottoms: I wanted to feel the floor under my feet, and grip it with my toes. Distracted by these thoughts, I lost my still precarious balance and sat down on the carpeted floor with a bump. The door of the closet was open. I caught sight of myself in the long mirror on the inside. Stella, our house-keeper, emerged from the darkness of the hallway. I was not seeing her but rather her reflection in the glass. And I saw that she was seeing the me that I saw in the glass; and I laughed, realizing for the first time that this was the me that others saw

"Pretty girl," Stella said, laughing with me. She lifted me up and wafted me through the air in her strong hands. I was ecstatic.

A sharply contrasting memory of approximately the same period followed close upon the first:

I pulled myself up by the leg of my crib, in the room I shared with a baby nurse named Miss Small, who was there for the first two years of my life. My mother was kneeling several feet away. She smiled painful encouragement, her arms outstretched. I let go of the crib leg, and, with a speed which precluded the need for balance, toddled toward her.

"So beautiful," she said with tears in her voice. She hugged me close to her. I didn't like being constrained. I whined and tried to wriggle free. Useless. I pushed my knees up between us. Finally, she released me, naming me with mingled hurt and accusation. I scowled, resisting the implications in her voice.

Malailly was the name of the park down the big hill, between Walton Avenue and Gerard Avenue. There was a playground with a large wading pool. The pool was empty, so it could not have been summer. The playground was nearly empty, so it was probably during school hours. I was about two. My mother pushed me from behind on one of the "baby swings", the kind with a movable bar in the front to prevent the child from falling out. My mother was pushing me from behind. I looked back to see what she was doing. I leaned forward to see the asphalt move under me. Then I leaned back and threw my head back, exhilarated by the infiniteness of pale sky combined with the motion. My mother stopped pushing. I swung my legs wildly and ineffectually, trying to keep the motion going. I whined my displeasure. My mother made soothing, then annoyed sounds as she struggled, successfully, to disengage me from the swing. She put me on the ground and walked in front of me. I was supposed to follow. Instead, I remained behind, and pushed one of the closer-to-the-ground "big children's" swings. But I was distracted by my mother's walking away. I forgot the swing I'd just pushed. Naturally, it smacked me on the rebound. The sharp pain took me by surprise. I howled. My mother, a few steps away, whirled around and whisked me up. She had assumed that my head had been hit, because that was her fear. I could not capture her attention to show her where the wound was, because she was completely absorbed in her own powerful emotion. Paradoxically, her concern for me made her inaccessible to me. My pain had been superseded by hers. My screams had subsided by the time we arrived at Dr. Cohn's office, where, for the first time, we all saw the large, surprisingly colorful welt on my shoulder.

Malailly Park again. I was three. It was summer, and I had just stepped out of the enormous, shallow swimming pool. It was only slightly concave, not really pool-like but rather a large nearly flat paved area surrounded by a brick border, with a high, spiked, black fence. Now that it was summer, its surface was covered with shallow water fed by a sprinkler system in the center. I ran from the pool to my mother to be enfolded in a fluffy, comforting bath towel. Once I was sufficiently warmed and dried, I was ready to run back to the pool.

"You have to change your suit," she said, "so you won't catch cold."

"I won't catch cold," I replied. "And I'm not going to change my suit outside. Nobody changes their clothes outside."

"Mothers get their children out of wet suits, if they care about their health," she hissed.

"No they don't," I yelled.

"Then we'll have to go home," she challenged.

"No I won't," I shouted.

"You can be swathed in towels," she offered. "No one will know you're getting out of one suit and into another."

"No," I yelled, as my mother grabbed me and yanked my shorts down.

"Everybody is looking at me," I screamed.

"That's because you're yelling," she said.

Enraged beyond verbalization, I screamed until the sound filled my consciousness, obliterating my mother and my humiliation.

The first Compulsion began when I was three. My mother would leave me on the toilet with instructions to have a bowel movement, and close the door behind her. She would be back to check.

In the meantime, I would pull a foot to my face and begin to bite one of the nails. It took some exploration, to find the right angle, but eventually my teeth would rip off a slice of nail. It felt good when it finally peeled free. If my mother returned while I was in the middle of biting a nail, I felt uncomfortable until I could finish the job. It was like having an unscratched itch or a piece of soot in the eye. And I never bit my toe nails when I was alone in bed at night, although it would seem to have been a perfect opportunity. That was because it was dark, which made it impossible to see what had been accomplished so far: my Compulsion was visual as well as being a kind of self-flagellation.

I can't remember the first time I bit my toenails, but I remember the last. I was four and, by this time, in charge of toileting myself. One day, I bit a slice of nail off the big toe of the right foot. I bit it so far down that the toe bled. I don't remember the pain, but I remember the panic, my frenzied attempt to staunch the blood and clean up every last drop that had dribbled onto the black and white tiled floor, obliterating the evidence. My toe felt fine when I left the bathroom. But the next morning, when my mother began to lace my shoe, I was in pain and could not avoid telling her. When she examined the toe, which looked worse than it did the day before, she, of course, asked me how it happened. I told her I stubbed it outside. My toenail-biting Compulsion was over, because the likelihood that I would be discovered was now too great. Instead, I took to biting my fingernails, like a "normal" anxious person, frequently gnawing the nails down so low that my fingers hurt and occasionally bled.

There are pictures of me at five or six, in a coat that was much too small. At the time it was taken, my father, who rarely remarked on anything about anybody, commented on it. The family joke was that you couldn't peel it off me.

My mother always took me clothes shopping in department stores. She said she preferred department stores to small owner-operated clothing shops, because she could return things, and also because she didn't feel obligated to buy if she didn't see anything she liked. I too liked department stores, but for other reasons. I liked the escalators. I enjoyed trying on ladies' hats and seeing how different each one made me look. What I didn't like was trying on clothes, especially coats, every coat in my size in every department store on Fifth Avenue, frequently more than once each, and having my mother feel to see if there was enough room (for her, not for me) in the shoulder, chest and waist, all with a pained expression on her face. It was the same possessiveness of my body which had enraged me when she yanked off my shorts, when I was three. So I would try to avoid the whole thing as long as possible. But inevitably, the day would come. And because I found the process of shopping with my mother excruciating, I would agree to any coat which met her standard, in order to end it. Even my agreement didn't end the process, because she was never quite sure she had made the very best possible choice, but it shortened it. Then I would get home to discover that I absolutely loathed the coat, and refuse to wear it for as long as possible.

"But you chose it," my mother would say, uncomprehendingly.

I felt that I had "chosen" it, in the sense that someone "chooses" to admit guilt under torture. Oddly, I almost always liked the way the coat looked and felt about a year after its purchase, when it actually fit me.

I began to weigh myself several times a day when I was six, which was when I first felt that my stomach was too big. I made no attempt to curb my appetite, especially for sweets, but weighed myself frequently, hoping I'd lose weight. I kept this Compulsion a secret from adults also, but shared it with my friend Isabel. In fact, going into the bathroom together and weighing ourselves became a shared, almost daily ritual. In order to be absolutely precise, we had to make sure the dial was set exactly on zero, and take off all of our clothing. Then we cheated, by moving around on the scale until we found the balance that recorded the lowest poundage. We kept the door unlocked, a requirement of my mother's when there was another child present. Which is why, one day, we were caught in the act by Stella, my parents' housekeeper, who proceeded to turn on the tub, and plunk us into it. Stella was laughing, and Isabel and I shrieked with glee.

Isabel and I continued to weigh ourselves regularly and competitively. I always weighed more, but I was three or four inches taller, and the pounds were prorated, so to speak. We argued about how many pounds each inch was worth. As we approached adolescence, we dieted, on the alternating feast and famine model. My diet, throughout high school, consisted of orange juice, skim milk and a piece of toast for breakfast, an apple for lunch, and steak and vegetables for dinner. Not surprisingly, I was always tired in the afternoon, which affected my social life more than my studies. I never had the energy to participate in after-school activities. On weekends I went wild eating, especially if I was with Isabel. Our feasts were, emotionally, like drunken orgies. Weight-wise, the alternation of dieting and voracious non-stop eating canceled each other out. My weight ranged between 100 and 105 pounds during my high school years. I was not Anorexic. My eating pattern, and the hyper concern with weight which provoked it, were certainly Disordered, but probably not unusually so. Actually, eating Disorders were the one type of Obsessive/Compulsive Spectrum Disorder that the members of the Tricotillomania group felt a kinship with, partly because three of the six of us had sisters who were–or had been–Anorexic. The two conditions, Tricotillomania and Anorexia, are alike in that both are body-focused Obsessive/Compulsive Spectrum Disorders, the 'Spectrum' being those mental Disorders, which are frequently ameliorated by antidepressants of the Selective Serotonin Reuptake Inhibitor variety. And, emotionally, both Anorexics and Tricotillomaniacs attempt to alleviate anxiety through controlling some aspect of our own bodies.

Four months after I joined the group, there was a Tricotillomania conference at McLean Hospital in Boston. I went there with Vivian and Carol in Carol's car. I soon became aware that Vivian and Carol were two of the most controlling people I had ever met. "Move here, move there, open the window, close the window, hand me this, hand me that." They wouldn't let me relax for a minute, which irritated me. My response was to disagree with their opinions, stated or implied, on any subject. This did not endear me to them. They ganged up on and ostracized me. It was like being catapulted back through the decades to childhood. Only it was more devastating then.

I remember one occasion when my two 'best friends,' Isabel and Judy, excluded me from a play date. When Isabel said "we're not going to play with you," I was plunged into a state of misery. Of course, I toughed it out, saying, "who cares about you?" Then I went home–to weep. I was walking through the dining room on my way to the kitchen, weeping and at the same time hoping Stella would give me a Malomar to assuage my unhappiness, when I was surprised by my father, who was sitting at the dining room table in his bathrobe, writing on a legal pad. Usually, my father worked in the bedroom that he and my mother shared.

"Stop crying," my father ordered. I was able to stop the vocalization, but not the tearing or sniffling.

"Why are you bawling like that," he sounded annoyed.

When I told him of my friends' betrayal, he said I shouldn't allow myself to care about what other kids thought or said. In fact, he told me that a good book was better than a friend. I disagreed vociferously.

I had been disconcerted by running into my father, while I was in a state of emotional upheaval. I wasn't surprised that he had virtually ordered me to squelch my display of emotion. If I'd known he was going to be in the dining room, I would have sought the privacy of my bedroom to cry in.

Tricotillomania Conference Interspersed With 'Inner Child' Work

When we arrived in Boston, Vivian told us she had definitely decided to stay with a cousin, who had extended an invitation to her when she'd called, telling him when she planned to be in Boston. I was glad that one of them was departing; I didn't care which. What I remembered from similar situations in childhood was that it takes two to ostracize a third. I was right. Carol's attitude toward me changed after Vivian left. The next few hours with Carol were pleasant. She became more relaxed, now that her anxiety wasn't being reinforced by Vivian's.

That night, in the anonymous hotel room, with Carol asleep in the next bed, I had a particularly riveting, multi-sensory visualization, one in which the adult seer became part of the play.

I watched my six year-old self jumping rope alone in front of the large six-story apartment building in which she lived.

She was plump, with long slender limbs and a delicately rounded, fine-featured face. Her blue eyes and orange hair were both exceptionally brilliant. Her expression was firm, almost pugnacious, as she concentrated on the rhythm of the rope, which encircled her. She counted jumps, determined to break her previous record for jumping without getting tripped up, which I was afraid would never happen. Finally it did, and I broke in before she could get started again.

"Jeni" I called. She turned toward me, first her eyes, then her head, finally her whole body. I followed Bradshaw's suggestion and told her I was from her future. She looked interested.

"Where can we sit down and talk?" I asked.

"Over there," she said, pointing to the park across the street. We walked to the corner, as she'd been taught, and crossed with the light. I didn't try to hold her hand because she had just recently begun crossing the street by herself, and definitely did not want to be "crossed" by an adult. I let her guide me. We climbed a small hill, then turned right to a semicircle of extremely wide, deep steps leading to what she called "the circle". In the middle of the circle was a stone fountain. And at the center of the fountain was a cylindrical stone structure surrounded by three mermaids separated by curved tables. She climbed onto a mermaid's lap, and from there, seated herself on one of the tables. I sat next to her on the table. We were snug in the center of the circle within a circle, at the north end of the one block by three block rectangle of the park. It was a chilly early dusk in late November. The park was nearly empty; there was no one else at that end of the park.

"How is life treating you?" I asked.

"OK," she answered, not looking at me, squirming, as children often do when being interrogated by adults.

"Jeni," I said, "look at me. I know something is bothering you. What is it?"

Her eyes still averted, she said sadly, "I never know if my friends really like me or not."

The mermaids began to laugh. I turned to find that they had become three friends of mine, Gloria, Millie, and Robin. I introduced them to Jeni. They said they were happy to meet her. I told them I'd be back and asked Jeni to come sit on the stone seat surrounding the mermaid circle. She agreed, and began to climb down from her perch. I had a desire to pick her up but squelched it. She was too dignified.

"My friends like you," I said.

"I don't care about what grown-ups think," she replied sharply. "I only care what kids think."

She was so ingenuous about letting me know who really counted.

"You don't think much of adults," I said.

"I wish my mother wouldn't lo-o-o-ove me so much."

"You sound sarcastic. Don't you think she loves you?"

"What she means by love is that I should appreciate how much she worries about me," Jeni replied.

"That's an odd definition for love. What do you think it is?"

"When you love someone," she said thoughtfully, "you want to be with them and tell them things that are fun, and follow each other's ideas." She was so definite in all she said, so secure in her opinions, in comparison with my adult self.

"What did you mean—you're from my future?" she took me by surprise. "Are you going to be my teacher?"

"No," I said. "What I meant was, you're going to be me in the future, in 45 years."

"How come you decided to visit me after all this time?" she asked.

"Because, no matter what happens or doesn't happen, I always seem to spend too much of my time being miserable. I think the worst of it was when I was in my teens. Well, there's a fad now called "inner-child work." You're supposed to see yourself at different ages and have conversations with your younger selves to find out how you got your present set of problems or "issues," as problems that go on and on are sometimes called. But I can see that you don't have many problems except for your fear that your friends will reject you."

"But that is a big problem," said Jeni. "It's an issue."

"Yes, it is," I agreed. "I won't make the mistake your father did, and tell you that a good book is better than a friend. There's nothing better than a good friend, except knowing how to be a good, loyal, honest friend to yourself."

I surmised from her disdainful expression that Jeni was not interested in such a concept.

"You sound like my mother," she accused. I can't ever let her know if I feel bad, because either she'll blame me for feeling bad, or else she'll try to make me do something I don't want to do that she thinks will make me forget about what I'm upset about."

And you don't want to be distracted from feeling bad?" I asked with some sarcasm.

Jeni was enraged. "I want the thing I feel bad about to change, you stupidhead," she yelled.

I came away from my interaction with my six-year-old self, realizing I'd forgotten the whole point of Bradshaw's inner-child work, which is to comfort and reassure one's former self. That's because, although she certainly could have used some reassurance about her appealingness to other children, my six-year-old self didn't trust and therefore couldn't use any approbation that came from adults.

Carol and I arrived at the conference the next morning, chilled by the freezing rain that pelted us on the way. We made plans to meet during the lunch break. Making plans to meet was necessary because of the numbers of people at the conference–about three hundred. There were very few men, and even fewer children. The vast majority of the attendees were adult women, which was not surprising since about 90% of those who have Tricotillomania are women. The group that seemed underrepresented to me was adolescent girls. The fact that Tricotillomania, like Anorexia, usually affects females, and, like Anorexia, usually begins in adolescence or soon thereafter indicates to me that these two Obsessive/Compulsive Spectrum Disorders have something to do with the psycho-social ramifications of becoming an adult female in this culture. Both of these Obsessive/Compulsive Spectrum Disorders begin as attempts to gain control over an aspect of one's body, in the face of terrifying feelings of powerlessness, ultimately provoking even more extreme feelings of powerlessness because of one's inability to control the Disorder.

When I was seven, I developed tics which involved the muscles of my jaw and neck, which I had to stretch and contract repeatedly. I also had vocal tics, throat clearing and coughing. In other words, I had simple Tourette Syndrome. I did not have extreme Tourette Syndrome. I didn't fling my arms and legs about, nor was I subject to uncontrollable cursing spells. Yet, I hesitate to call what I had "mild". That's because it was torture. It was intolerable being in my skin. My mother took me to a psychiatrist. I was told that he was a doctor, which he was, but not that he was a psychiatrist. So of course, I was suspicious. What kind of doctor was this, who didn't have a tongue depressor or a stethoscope? I refused to answer his questions, which mostly concerned my feelings about my parents. I did reveal myself inadvertently, through a drawing of birds, in which I used only the black crayon. At home my birds were always yellow, my favorite color. I remember the doctor telling my mother (as if I couldn't hear), "she's more troubled than she appears."

My father didn't think I needed psychiatry. He thought that all I needed was the will power to quit distorting my face and growling. If my father was there when I began ticking, he would order me to stop. I would have given anything to be able to stop; it was torture. But I couldn't. And my father would go livid and speak in that low, menacing voice.

"Stop it," he'd hiss. and when I didn't stop, "go to your room." I was outraged that I was being punished, that I had incurred my father's hostility for something I had no control over. It didn't occur to me till many years later that my father had facial tics and throat clearing that were very similar to mine. It was a case of disowning a behavior he loathed in himself.

At the age of nine, I had large protruding front teeth and canines of which Dracula would have been proud. I was crushed when the dentist said he wouldn't consider putting braces on my teeth until I was at least 12. I couldn't face living with such teeth for three years. So, every day, I spent time in the bathroom, pulling my teeth back in with a string. My self-orthodonture seemed to be working. Or else my jaw was simply expanding to accommodate my teeth. In any case, checking on and "fixing" my teeth became compulsive. I never told anyone about it, and invariably explained my frequent, extended stays in the bathroom by saying I had a stomach ache. This was never questioned. My mother thought I was constipated, and urged me to eat a great deal of fruit.

It was spring, and I was about to turn 10. I was plump around the middle, with long slender limbs: the Eloise body. My hair was long and wild, my expression a habitual scowl, though I was not unhappy at the moment. Isabel and I were together in the park across the street, the park with the mermaid circle.

"Look," Isabel said. We stopped to stare at two teens making out on a bench. "Ooooo, they're, kissing," said Isabel, loudly enough for them to hear.

"Their tongues are touching," I observed even more loudly. We both began to make vomiting sounds, very authentic, and after several simulated regurgitations the girl was unable to ignore us. We could see the color rising in her face. When she could no longer contain her discomfort, she pulled away from the boy and eyed us crossly. The boy was angry too, and (thrillingly) decided to act. He rose from the bench and approached us. At that point, we turned on our heels, ran and giggled–giggled and ran, glancing over our shoulders from time to time. We stopped running when it became clear that we were not being pursued. But we continued to chortle and screech for several minutes, delighted with the effect we had produced.

Twenty years later, in a Consciousness Raising Group, I realized how much sense our antagonism made. It was based on seeing how people were taken over by sexuality after puberty, their lives subsumed by their sexual roles. It seemed inevitable: one day you wake up, and you've forgotten who you are.

When I was 13, my parents, my younger sister and I, along with my father's two sisters and their doctor husbands, were vacationing at the Traymore hotel in Atlantic City, in late December. I was lonely, because I did not having any contemporaries to communicate with (my little sister was five). But there was solace: the skating rink, glinting white and inviting in the sunlight, or illuminated by electric lights contrasting brilliantly with the darkness of evening. For half an hour a day, I had figure skating lessons. I wanted the lessons, although, deep down, I knew they were futile, too late, because I had already reached adult height, and with it a concern about falling. What I loved was simply gliding round and round, listening to the pop tunes playing over the loud speaker, while feeling the rhythmic motion of my body and the coolness rising from the ice. I had spent the afternoon skating, and was still exhilarated when I returned to the hotel to bathe and change before dinner. Then, instantly, everything was grotesquely transformed by the moist, brilliant red stain on the crotch of my underpants, which I wrapped in toilet paper and disposed of in the waste basket. Then I let the water out of the tub, and put on fresh underpants, the crotch much reinforced with wads of toilet paper. I knew this expedient would not suffice for long, that I would have to tell my mother in order to get a Kotex. Why oh why couldn't this have waited until we were home, where I could simply have filched a sanitary napkin from my mother's box? I cringed to think that my mother might very well tell my aunts, who would of course tell my uncles, who, because they were doctors, were privileged to know everyone's most intimate bodily events. I wished I could disappear and never be seen by any of my relatives ever again.

The summer I was 14, Isabel and I went to Deerwood music camp. We had both begun piano lessons at eight. My progress had been desultory or non-existent, while Isabel had become a serious music student, attending classes at Julliard. In fact, I had no desire to play the piano, although I had signed up for a once-a-week lesson. But I had discovered a compelling interest in modern dance. It was worth rising early on a cold Adirondack morning to dance under the supervision of Donny McCale, who was wonderful to watch and to follow. I didn't even mind his criticism. On the contrary, I was happy, knowing that his attention meant he thought I had a talent worth whipping into shape. And I liked Deerwood, because, although we were expected to be disciplined in pursuing music, dance, drama, or the choral singing that we were all required to participate in every evening, the rest of our time was free. Twice a week, Isabel and I had horseback riding lessons, which I loved. On other afternoons we swam or played casual volleyball. There was none of the competitive sportsmanship I'd loathed at other summer camps. One afternoon in July I'd decided that it was time to write the obligatory weekly letter to my parents. But I didn't write it—at least, not that afternoon.

I can see myself enter the bunk, which I shared with seven other girls and a counselor. For some reason, I was furtive, glancing around to make sure no one was there. Heading straight for the mirror over the sinks in the common bathroom at the back of the bunk, I gazed at my face critically. I liked the way my cheekbones had expanded; my upper and lower face were now in proportion with each other. I liked my pale skin, though I wished it wasn't freckled. Still, I was grateful that I didn't have acne like Isabel. I loathed the brilliant orange color of my hair, though I liked its texture: thick, moderately coarse, and wavy. What I disliked the most were my lashes, which were so pale as to appear non-existent, although my fingers told me that they were reasonably long and thick. I wished I had mascara, but I didn't. I thought that perhaps if I curled the lashes and put Vaseline on them, they would be visible. I walked back into the bedroom part of the bunk, knowing I'd seen an eyelash curler somewhere. My eyes lit on it. Pressed by an intense inner need, I did not care who the curler belonged to. I grabbed a jar of Vaseline from another dresser. Back to the mirror. I put the Vaseline on the sink and grasped the curler firmly in my right hand. Leaning over the sink, so that my face was as close to the mirror as possible, I raised the curler to my right eye.

"No!" my contemporary self screamed to my adolescent incarnation. "Don't do it!"

She did not hear me. She was much too intent on what she was doing to pick up a voice from another dimension. So I was forced to watch her/me make the insignificant error which would hold me prisoner for decades to come.

Unfortunately, I had neglected to insert the rubber pad into the bottom of the curler, so that instead of curling the lashes, the instrument I pulled away from my face held half of the lashes from my right lid and had twisted the remaining lashes so that they stuck out at odd angles. For the first time, I really saw my lashes, and they were a mess. I thought I would remedy the situation by tweezing out the offending remaining lashes and, to that end, picked up a tweezer from a bathroom shelf. I tweezed out the rest of the lashes from my right lid, and then, though there was nothing wrong with them, I pulled out several lashes from the left lid for the sake of symmetry.

I had planned to swim later that afternoon, but now I didn't want to. In fact, I didn't want to do anything.

All this time, the years between then and now, I identified with the "I" who made the mistake. My punishment was to spend countless hours attempting (always unsuccessfully) to correct it. I alternated plucking out lashes and sticking the remaining lashes together, first with the Vaseline that was available at the time, later with mascara, trying to camouflage the expanses of bare lid. And I was afraid that someone would get close enough to me to notice and comment on my mangled lashes. What would I say? In school, between classes, I inevitably headed for the mirror in the girls' bathroom. After making certain I was alone, I checked the almost nonexistent lashes of the right lid. Then I moved them around with my fingers, trying to make them more evenly spaced. I knew they wouldn't stay where I placed them: they never did. But day after day, month after month, year after year, I tried, doggedly, incomprehensibly. If I heard someone entering the room, I panicked and quickly stepped away from the mirror, pretending to be fixing my hair.

I didn't take my instruments of torture–tweezers, mascara, and cold cream–to school. But once home, I ensconced myself in the bathroom for hours, plucking out "wrong" lashes, then sticking the remaining lashes together with mascara.

"It's a mess," I'd think. "Now I have to remove the mascara and begin again." My sister complained that I spent too long in the bathroom we shared. I always used the excuse of a stomach ache. After I'd been pressured out of the bathroom, I continued my futile activity behind a mirrored closet door in my bedroom. The placement of the door was ideal: I could see myself and, at the same time, not be seen by someone entering the room. The drawback of this arrangement was the lack of a water supply. Eventually, the discomfort caused by the cold cream and mascara in my eye forced me to return to the bathroom.

From time to time, my mother entered my room unannounced while I was "fixing" my lashes. I would come out from behind the mirror, annoyed at being prevented from completing whatever aspect of the Obsessive/Compulsive process I was engaged in.

"What is it?" I'd say.

"I want to speak with you," she'd respond.

"There's nothing to discuss," I'd counter, wanting to get rid of her.

"But I'm your mother," she'd insist, stating the obvious.

"So what," I'd reply belligerently, desperately willing her to leave, because my right lid was stinging like crazy, and I was not about to reveal my suffering to her. That was something I didn't even want to contemplate.

I was abruptly pulled from my reminiscences, when a woman said, "excuse me," to make me aware that she wanted pass me to get to a seat farther down the row I was sitting in. I stood to let her pass, and then decided I wanted to walk around a bit, since the conference hadn't yet begun.

Most of the women had long hair, often elaborately coifed, like Carol's. I spotted a few wigs and a few women with who'd tied scarves around their heads, as I did at that time. I also noticed and felt elated at seeing many women either lashless or with damaged lashes. Ever since I'd begun torturing and tweezing out my lashes, I'd used the opportunity of close proximity to so many people offered by the New York subways to see if anyone else besides me lacked a full set of lashes. Standing, I could view the lashes of an entire row of seated riders surreptitiously. (I'd discovered two in all those years of checking.) At the conference, I found I was doing lash checking more or less openly. And for the first time in all those years, I was not afraid that someone would notice my own damaged lashes and ask, "What happened to your eyelashes?" Actually, no one had ever asked that of me, but the fear of it was ever-present. It occurred to me that from now on, if anyone asked me about my missing lashes, I would simply tell them the truth: that I have a Disorder that impels me to pull them out.

The presentations of the professional speakers at the conference were academic and research oriented, in contrast with the professional presentations I'd heard at Stacey's weekly 'showcase for therapists,' which was treatment oriented. That was because the conference, unlike Stacey's series, was being given for the benefit of professionals, as well as sufferers. For me the academic presentations were balm. They allowed me to be detached, outside the Disorder, looking in.

Two of the conference presentations were by sufferers. One, Christina Dubowsky, was a great spokesperson representing Trichotillomaniacs. She was energetic, practical and purposeful, like the other women I'd known whose sole Compulsion was hair pulling. And she clearly presented herself as someone coping with the Disorder, not cured of it. She put us in touch with the pain of our out-of-control self-destructiveness, to tell us that what we were doing now, confronting the problem through connectedness with others who share it, was the most important single factor in alleviating the pain. And I have found that to be true, *regardless of whether or not that connectedness ameliorates symptoms.* She told us about the Tricotillomania Learning Center, which she'd organized in California, where she runs assisted support groups and publishes a newsletter called *'In Touch,'* which features articles by professionals as well as personal stories by people with Tricotillomania. Christina was magnetic, drawing me and many others to introduce ourselves to her during the lunch break.

The other speaker/sufferer was one of the few men there, aside from the professionals. He had organized a 12-step group for people with OCD, Tricotillomania, and other Spectrum Disorders in Boston. He said that what he loved most was participating in sports. He'd injured his shoulder, playing touch football. But in spite of knowing that what he was doing was preventing the shoulder from healing, he could not stop pulling out his hair. Even the fear that his perpetual pulling might result in a permanent disability was not enough to stop him. But it was enough to send him to a therapist, who taught him behavior modification exercises which worked for him.

Not long after the conference, I slipped on ice and broke my right wrist. The following night with a cast extending from my hand to my elbow, with only the fingers free, I spent about two hours cutting my lashes in spite of the danger to both my wrist and my eye. Then I thought of the young athlete who spoke at the conference. I did not cut my lashes after that, although I continued to cut the hair on my head (an even more difficult contortion) all through the period that I wore the cast. The wrist took about three years to become completely normal. I don't know to what extent the hours of hair-cutting, straining a wrist that should have been kept as immobile as possible, contributed to the slowness of the healing. Still, on balance, I consider the accident fortuitous, coming soon after the conference as it did. It was this combination of events which led directly to letting go of the most entrenched of my compulsive urges: checking and depilating my lids, and then attempting to camoflage the bare expanses of lid with cosmetics.

The hair cutting didn't begin till much, much later: November of '86. I was with Joel at the apartment he shared with Dan. Joel's boyfriend, Henry, was there, and his friend, Kimball. We were all there for Joel, who was just been diagnosed with AIDS. Joel looked me in the eye and said, "Jeni, I'm going to die." We clung to each other and wept uncontrollably for a long time. My mind could not contain it. Although I hadn't drunk alcohol for over three years, I reached for one of the fifths of vodka that Kimball had brought. I poured some into a glass and drank it. I poured another, and another, desperately trying to blot out the unbearable knowledge. It wasn't working or maybe it was. When I returned home at 3 am, I was sober, but with a splitting headache, which was certainly a distraction. From habit, I began to look at my face in the mirror, to torture myself over my lashes, and the lumps and folds around my eyes that had been created by years of abrasive action. And now, my whole face was so swollen from alcohol and weeping, I couldn't bear to look at it. I looked at my hair instead. Rich, thick, brilliantly orange, it exploded into a high pompadour on top of my head. It was slicked back on the sides and reached the base of my neck in back.

My head throbbed painfully. I had to do something. I picked up a sewing shears and attacked my hair—recklessly, destructively. Within half an hour, I was almost bald—and exhausted. Finally, I was able to lose myself in sleep.

And of course, it didn't stop there. Hair cutting became an alternative Compulsion, one which was much more noticeable than its predecessor. Over the next several years, my various degrees of baldness drew exclamatory remarks (e.g. "What have you done to your hair!") as well as sympathy from friends, who had been unable to understand my extreme concern with my lashes. (Almost everyone cares about hair.)

It was movement, which in itself was positive. It made me much more aware that I had a mental Disorder, rather than a hair Disorder, even while I was caught up in it. And it led to finding help, through literature, lectures, support groups, and therapy.

Doctor Katherine Phillips

My experience in the Trichotillomania group had made me feel that Trichotillomania was an incomplete diagnosis for me. Their hair pulling, as they described it, was an out-of-control Compulsion, what the literature calls an Impulse Control Disorder. In contrast, my hair cutting, having begun as an exuberantly destructive (impulsive) act, had become a rigidly controlled perfectionistic ritual. Every hair on the right side had to be even with every other hair. And though countless hours of cutting might lead to a temporary resolution, I was only released from my endless labor until the next time I caught myself in a reflecting surface.

My therapist, David Miller, had been skeptical about my need for a diagnosis, because people with Obsessive/Compulsive type Disorders need to learn to keep breathing while they're in limbo, and the desperation of my need for a definite label did partake of that OCDish, "If I only had this one essential piece of information, everything would become clear to me (and I could be at peace)." On the other hand, a precise diagnosis can be a great help in designing successful behavior modification exercises. I had tried behavior mod techniques designed to alleviate Tricotillomania, and they hadn't worked, hadn't made sense to me.

I read an article by a Dr. Katherine Phillips about what she termed Body Dysmorphic Disorder (BDD). In the article, she mentions a patient who spent eight hours a day cutting her hair; and there was no mention of Tricotillomania. I thought that the reason Dr. Phillips called this woman's Disorder Body Dismorphic Disorder, **not** Tricotillomania, was because she always cut her hair in front of a mirror, with the purpose of making the hair symmetrical. Her case was very similar to mine, in that the main focus of this client was visual, rather than tactile.

Dr. Phillips writes, that the purpose of visual checking in BDD is to allay anxiety, to reassure, though it frequently has the opposite effect. True. The looking lets you know just how awful it is: you don't have to wonder. And for those Body Dysmorphics who have associated compulsive behaviors, in addition to checking, it may mean that you'll be stuck for hours in repeated failed attempts to correct or camouflage the perceived flaw, until you are either satisfied or exhausted.

I also read an article by Drs. Phillips and Hollander which relates how BDD was classified in the past. It was once called Beauty Hypochondria. In its 'delusional' form it has been classified as a psychosis. Drs. Phillips and Hollander disagree with its classification as two Disorders, one delusional and one not, because, according to them, the same individual over time often has varying degrees of 'insight' about the reality of the 'imagined' flaw They also stated that there may in fact be a minor flaw. Actually, with respect to the few BDD sufferers I've encountered, I could always see what they were talking about. So the concept of delusion vs. insight into the existence of the flaw doesn't really seem relevant to me. What is relevant in cases of Body Dismorphic Disorder are the intensity and pervasiveness of the concern about a minor imperfection, the ways in which it gobbles up time, energy, life.

"Dysmorphia," Hollander and Phillips wrote, "is a Greek word for ugliness."

And the Disorder now classified as Body Dismorphic Disorder was at one time called Dysmorphobia, which would mean fear of ugliness, since phobias generally refer to fears. For me, the term "Dysmorphobia "is more descriptive than the current "Body Dismorphic Disorder," because what I experience before I actually examine the flaw is that fear.

Drs. Phillips and Hollander's article also discusses Depersonalization Disorder. Their reasoning, with respect to writing about BDD and Depersonalization Disorder in the same article, seems to be that they are both body-focused Disorders, which are somehow related to OCD. I couldn't see that the article makes any plausible connection between BDD and Depersonalization Disorder, and didn't think there was one, until I remembered having had a couple of episodes of Depersonalization Disorder during the first year of my marriage. So, yes, I did think there was a connection, though I wasn't quite sure what it was.

In any case, I was sufficiently excited and intrigued by Dr. Phillips's insight into Body Dysmorphic Disorder to write to her:

September 10, 1993

Dear Dr. Phillips,

I'm writing to you with respect to your article, "Body Dysmorphic Disorder: The Distress Of Imagined Ugliness," and with respect to the article you co-authored with Dr. Hollander, "Body Image And Experience Disorders."

I have suffered with Body Dysmorphic Disorder for 38 years (since the onset of puberty). I have only recently begun to get a handle on my Disorder, through Obsessive/Compulsive and Tricotillomania support groups, Cognitive/Behavioral therapy and (for the past two months) Prozac.

I am currently writing a book about my experience of BDD, the therapies I have used to combat it, and the quality of the results. And because you have the most comprehensive understanding of this Disorder that I have encountered, I would like to discuss some things pertaining to it with you.

First of all, intuition tells me that you are correct in perceiving a strong similarity (perhaps an identity) between BDD and OCD. Although I do not have any OCD symptoms, I find that it is easy for me to understand by analogy the concerns (Obsessions) and endless compulsiveness of people with OCD. You differentiate between the "Obsessions" of OCD and the "Overvalued Ideas" of BDD. I wish that you would clarify this distinction for me.

I was especially interested in your mention of a patient who spent 8 hours a day cutting her hair in an attempt to achieve a certain aesthetic effect. I would have thought you were talking about me, except that I know we've never met. Actually, my Disorder began with my pulling out lashes with a tweezer, switched to cutting the lashes and eventually involved the skin around the (right) eye and the hair on my head, particularly the hairline above the right eye. It was also the "eight hours" that I related to. I have done even longer stretches than that, cutting, cutting, cutting. And because my Disorder primarily involves hair removal, I'd assumed that it was some sort of blend of BDD and Tricotillomania. But in your article you don't mention Tric with regard to the haircutter. In my own case, my compulsive checking is frequently manual as well as visual.

I was also interested in your discussion of the Japanese and Korean literature on BDD, in which it is considered a form of Social Phobia, thus emphasizing the interpersonal aspect of the Disorder. You write about patients who wanted, above all, to avoid having others see their defect. Fortunately, this has not been my problem. In fact, in my youth, I was narcissistic, and even exhibitionistic. However, I have always been isolated, largely (as with OCD sufferers) because of the amount of time that my Compulsions demanded. You do mention narcissism as something which may coexist with (or be an aspect of) BDD. The two tendencies, narcissism and hiding out of fear of having one's defect discovered seem, on the surface at least, to be opposites. I would like your thought on this apparent contradiction.

You say that Body Dysmorphic Disorder has been considered an Affective Spectrum Disorder. I know that affect is emotion, but I'm not clear about how this pertains to BDD specifically.

I would really appreciate some feedback from you on any or all of these subjects.

I received a form letter. It said:

Dear Ms. Wolf,

Thank you very much for your recent letter. I receive a very large number of personal letters and am unfortunately unable to respond to all of them in person. I am, however, enclosing some information on BDD, which I hope you find helpful. I would strongly encourage you if you or a loved one is suffering from Depression, Anxiety, Body Dysmorphic Disorder or other body image concerns or any emotional distress to see a psychiatrist in person for an evaluation. Being seen in person by a professional would be far more valuable than any advice that I could give you by letter. If you would like to see me for an evaluation, I would be very happy to do so. You could arrange for an evaluation by calling and speaking to Amy or Janet, our intake personnel. If, because of distance from McLean, this does not prove feasible, I would suggest that you see a psychiatrist in your area. If you think you suffer from BDD but cannot find a psychiatrist in your area who specializes in this Disorder, I would suggest that you see someone who specializes in OCD, which has similarities to BDD. Again, if your situation is particularly difficult and you would like to see me for a consultation, I would be happy to see you.

I should have been forewarned. I mean, even if she didn't have the time to answer (any of) my questions, at least she—or an assistant—could have deleted parts that did not apply, like telling me to see a professional. My letter clearly stated that I was in Cognitive/Behavioral therapy (most widely recommended for both OCD and BDD) and that I was taking Prozac, indicating that I was seeing a psychiatrist. If she'd only read my address at the top of the page, a Manhattan address, she would have realized I'd have no problem finding a specialist in anything.

Unfortunately, all I saw was the "If you would like to see me for an evaluation, I would be very happy to do so." I called and made an appointment. The intake report, which I received right before I saw Dr. Phillips pretty much got my story straight, including the fact that I had been in therapy. Only the last line of the first paragraph was jarring. It said, "the problem she has is that she pulls out clumps of her hair," which I never did and certainly never said that I did.

The intake report also recorded my request to use a tape recorder so I would not forget what I was told with regards to treatment. Unfortunately, although presumably Dr. Phillips received the intake report some days before my appointment—it is dated 3/21/94, and my appointment was for 3/30/94—she never responded to that request. I did not bring a tape recorder, but, as I recall, she made no specific suggestions about treatment, except to tell me I should avail myself of regular professional treatment. I, of course, informed her that I already was in treatment and had been for some time, with minimal improvement. I told her that I had come all the way from Manhattan to Boston, because her articles indicated to me that she had a great deal of insight about BDD, so I wanted her to do an evaluation of my case.

I was in Dr. Phillips's office for almost three hours. I talked and talked, while she took notes almost continuously. Her questions were few, but relevant. She was a catalyst for provoking vivid, detailed memories of my Disorder at its worst:

When I went off to the University of Chicago in the fall of '59. I was exultant, euphoric. This was the moment I had been waiting for: escape from the restrictions imposed by my parents, as well as from the oppression of perpetually reenacting what was expected by family, friends, schoolmates, everyone. I would do what I wanted to do and be what I wanted to be. I was very naive in thinking that I had a blank slate. In fact, I discovered that I knew almost nothing about what I should do with my freedom, how I could use it advantageously. For so long, "freedom" had been a goal, like "living happily ever after," whereas freedom is actually a practice, the practice of making decisions, evaluating the results, making corrections, evolving. And what about the problem with my eyelashes, which consumed hours of each day? I didn't think about that at all. That is, I didn't "officially" recognize that it was ongoing.

During the school terms, living in a dormitory, I had been subjected to a curfew. After the end of the spring term, for several days I was alone. The other students and the house matron had departed, so there was no one to enforce a curfew. Alone, with a complete absence of external oppression, I used the opportunity to oppress myself, to imprison and torture myself more totally and absolutely than ever before–or since. I would awaken late in the morning, look at all of the things that had to be sorted out and either packed up or discarded before returning to my parents' home in New York. I became overwhelmed, not knowing where to begin, and fled into the bathroom at the end of the hall. I had assumed that my ritual with tweezers and mascara would be simpler, when I didn't have to run into one of the stalls for cover because another resident had entered the room. It didn't work out that way. Freedom from fear of exposure and from the more generalized communal pressure to behave like a normal person and go to class or to dinner had, in fact, limited the amount of time given over to my Compulsion. Now, rather than two or three hours a day, it consumed 10, 12, 14 hours at a stretch. I was completely in its thrall.

I could visualize myself in my room in the dorm, the room I'd shared with Lynn until a few days earlier. Silence. Everyone had gone for the summer. The room was a wreck. Clothes, books, records, papers: everything was strewn about. I did not know where to begin. Instead, I escaped to the bathroom at the end of the hall. There was no competition for the mirror now, and no fear of discovery. I brought a tweezers, mascara, cold cream, and a towel. First, I creamed off the mascara that I was wearing, and rubbed it off with the towel, which made large dark stains. I stared at my right eye, at the lashes on my upper lid. I had not left many, but I could see at least two that were growing down and 'needed' to be tweezed out. Grabbing a particular lash was difficult, a challenge, fraught with tension, agonizing.

"Please don't let me make a mistake and tweeze out one of the "good ones," I thought. Because no matter how many I pulled out, I "had to" keep at it until I got the "bad ones." That was the rule. On the particular occasion I was remembering, I was lucky on my first pull. But getting the second "bad" lash was not easy. I pulled out three "good" ones in the process, my heart sinking lower with each new mistake. Finally, I grabbed the offending lash. Then I began to paste the remaining lashes together with clumps of mascara, trying desperately to make it appear that I had a full set of lashes. But no. It was a mess. It wouldn't do. I creamed the mascara off and began again. I repeated this process until my right lid was inflamed. But what concerned me more than the physical discomfort was that I was running out of mascara. This was my last shot, so it would have to suffice. I began that day's torture at four in the afternoon (I was waking up later and later). It was now two in the morning. I dressed in black and white striped denim pants and a sleeveless white cotton shirt. I put my keys, a pack of cigarettes, and half a bottle of Chianti from the night before into my shoulder bag and bounded down the stairs, out the door and into the street, finally released from my self-imposed prison. The street was empty. I was as completely isolated now as I had been for the past 10 hours. But now I was free to move, to breathe in the soothing summer night air, to get drunk, and to let my mind wander along with my feet.

Once I began to tackle the sorting and packing, I was no longer overwhelmed by it and the process went quickly. That breaking through into an activity had been a problem for me since high school, when I was thrust into a more rigorous and much more competitive academic environment.

"I can see clearly," I told Dr. Phillips, "–now that there is no longer a film of cold cream blurring my vision–that it was the resentment of the pressure, not the work itself, much of which I enjoyed, that created the blockage. It's the resentment of the necessity of performing an activity that paralyses my will, creating a kind of vacuum which my Obsession and attendant Compulsions rush in to fill."

Then, I visualized myself on the day of my return to Chicago in the fall of 1960. The first person I saw was a man I had known and fantasized about the year before. Everything clicked. We spent the night together....and the next....and the next. I still had my dorm room, and most of my time in the dorm, I spent doing my Compulsions, checking and pulling out lashes and then attempting to camoflage the resulting disaster with mascara. But I was spending most nights in the apartment that my lover shared with two other men. I could not spend endless time in the bathroom there, nor could I pursue my self torture in sight of my lover–or anyone else. I was able to squelch the perpetual need to check on my lashes, pluck out offending ones and attempt to camouflage the mess I'd created, knowing I'd be free to succumb to it the following afternoon.

I switched from brown mascara to navy blue shadow, which made my blue eyes look turquoise. The change from mascara to shadow was an improvement, because with the shadow I could blend the lashes into the lid. One problem with mascara was that I would have to clean it off my lid and, in so doing, would disturb the stuck-together lashes and have to begin again. Shadow was easier, a bit less tortured, but still extremely time consuming. I was still tweezing and filling in the bald spots, helplessly repeating the same error over and over and desperately attempting to fix it.

After four months of cohabitation, my lover and I married. Both before and after the wedding, our relationship was both intense and extremely time consuming, and created a significant diversion from my Obsessions and Compulsions. But my Obsessive/Compulsive Disorder was still there, waiting to claim me when my mind was not intensely absorbed in something else–and sometimes even then. I could not bear to have my new husband discover my Disorder any more than I could have borne exposure by my dorm mates, or my mother. Secrecy, now, as before, required the constant production of excuses for why I spent so long in the bathroom.

I became pregnant (it turned out) at approximately the time of the wedding. I looked forward to the baby. And the pregnancy gave me an excuse to simply drop the courses, which I was, in any case, flunking. It was a relief. We married in January. In July we traveled East in the second-hand car we'd bought with gifts from my parents, aunts, and uncles, and visited my parents at a resort in upstate New York. I had married thinking that my husband would rescue me, permanently, from my parents. Now I could see that he had no intention of doing that. To the contrary, his object was to draw closer to my parents, to pander to them, in order to exploit my father financially. Family was closing in on me, with no hope of escape. I began to experience "depersonalization." That is: other people did not appear real to me. They seemed to be merely fixtures in the world I inhabited. This provided a respite from the pain of feeling irrevocably trapped. The disadvantage of the state was that I hadn't a clue about others' motivations. Interpersonal relations became a mine field; I didn't know what people would say or do, or how they would react to what I said and did.

When my son Jonathan was born on October 2, 1961, it seemed to me that we were the only two real people in the world. The first time I held him, four hours after he was born, he held up his own head and gazed into my eyes with infinite love. He reminded me of a Buddha, full of joy, and completely present and available to the moment. Once, on an infrequent visit with my parents, when Jon was three, I took him to the park across from the solid, white brick building I'd grown up in, the park in which I'd spent so much of my own childhood. He surveyed the (to him) unfamiliar scene with pleasure and excitement.

"Look at all my friends," he said exultantly.

How different, I thought, from my own attitude. Even at the age three, I was skeptical about the positive potential of human interaction. I felt truly blessed to have a child, who anticipated human interaction with joy.

When Dr. Phillips said our time together was up–after almost three hours–I asked her for a diagnosis. She said that she wanted to consult with a Dr. O'Sullivan and would get in touch with me. A month passed, then two, and I didn't hear from her. I wrote to her. No response. After another month, I wrote to her again. Nothing. By this time, I was angry. Why was she behaving so irresponsibly? I decided to address her in an open letter to Jim Broach, Director of the Obsessive/Compulsive Foundation, which publishes a bi-monthly newsletter. I thought Dr. Phillips would be bound to see it there, and maybe I'd get a response from her. The following is the letter I sent.

Dear Dr. Phillips,

I write this 'open letter' to you, because you have not responded to the (2) letters I sent you directly.

By the winter of '94, I had reached a point of acute desperation in my attempt to control/alleviate my Disorder, which involved endless mirror checking and hair cutting. I had participated in support groups on a regular basis. I had also been in (Cognitive/Behavioral) therapy, both individual and group, and had availed myself of the services of a psycho pharmacologist specializing in OCD. None of the aforementioned had resulted in major, lasting improvement.

I read three articles of yours and was tremendously impressed with your insight into the nature of OCD and OC Spectrum Disorders, especially Body Dysmorphic Disorder. In fact your articles had confirmed my suspicion that BBD was an aspect of my problem. I made arrangements to have a session with you. (Geographic distance prevented my considering becoming a regular patient of yours.)

I had thought I would take notes on our session, which was on March 30, 1994 at McLean Hospital. Instead, all of my energies were focused on an effort to respond fully to your memory-provoking questions. I remember that you took extensive notes as I spoke. I have no criticism of the procedure I have described thus far. Unfortunately, for me, the process was incomplete. I received no benefit from whatever you gleaned from my response to your questions. I had asked for a diagnosis. You said you would consult with Dr. O'Sullivan and let me know. I wrote to you twice asking for a diagnosis and whatever other conclusions you had reached. I received no response from you. I did get a lengthy questionnaire from your clinic, which reinforced the impression that I was being treated not as a patient or client, but rather as a research subject. I shouldn't have had to pay $200 for that.

Jim Broach didn't publish my letter, but did send it to Dr. Phillips. This was the letter I received in response:

Dear Jenifer,

I recently received a copy of your letter from Jim Broatch, which he was kind enough to forward to me. I was sorry to learn that you had sent me several letters to which I did not respond. Unfortunately, as far as I can recall, I didn't receive your letters. Although I can't be certain of the reason, it may be that you sent them to me after I had left McLean Hospital and that they weren't forwarded to me.

I was also sorry to read that you didn't find your consultation helpful. My recollection is that we spent several hours together and that we had discussed my impressions and treatment options at some length, but it sounds as though this isn't what your experience was. I also recall having spoken to Dr. O'Sullivan and attempting to reach you by telephone to convey his impressions, but my recollection is that I wasn't successful in reaching you. I apologize for not having further pursued reaching you. I should also note that because of the atypical nature of your symptoms, I did not include you in my research series. All the information I obtained from you was solely for the purpose of your evaluation.

Although it's been some time since I saw you, I would be happy to speak with you about your consultation in the hope that you would find it helpful.

When we spoke a week later, I agreed that we'd spent several hours together. I reminded her that when I saw her, I hadn't any need for information about treatment options. In fact, I had attended a weekly group (Stacie's) which was a forum for all of the major New York practitioners in the field of OCD and OC Spectrum Disorders. Also, as I recalled, the whole session had been taken up with my recounting some of the history of my Disorder. We hadn't really discussed her impressions, which was why I had wanted an evaluation from her afterwards. And, though I didn't pursue the topic further, I felt that her assertion that she hadn't used her notes from the session in her research because I was an atypical case, though doubtless true, rather begged the question of intention. Still, the conversation I had with Dr. Phillips did resolve much of the antagonism I'd felt toward her.

Diagnosis

I was still frustrated with respect to having a firm diagnosis, so I decided to look up the diagnostic criteria for Obsessive/Compulsive Disorder, Obsessive/Compulsive Spectrum Disorders, Body Dysmorphic Disorder, and Trichotillomania in the current *Diagnostic And Statistical Manual Of Mental Disorders* (DSM 4) to see where my Disorder(s) fit in.

This is what I found for Obsessive/Compulsive Disorder, which is listed as an Anxiety Disorder: (1) The Obsessions are recurrent and persistent thoughts, impulses, or images that are experienced, at some time during the disturbance, as intrusive, and, that cause anxiety or distress. (2)The thoughts, impulses, or images are not simply excessive worries about real-life problems. (3) The person attempts to suppress such thoughts, etc., or to neutralize them with some other thought or action. (4) The person recognizes that the Obsessional thoughts, etc. are the product of his or her own mind (not imposed from without as in thought insertion). The Compulsions are (1) repetitive behaviors (handwashing, ordering, checking) or mental acts (praying, counting, repeating a word or words silently) that a person feels driven to perform in response to an Obsession, or according to rules that must be applied rigidly. (2)the behaviors or mental acts are aimed at preventing or reducing distress or preventing some dreaded event or situation; however, these behaviors or mental acts either are not connected in a realistic way with what they are designed to neutralize or prevent or are clearly excessive. DSM 4 also says that a diagnosis of OCD is not warrented if the symptoms can be accounted for by other "Axis 1 Disorders," which are called Clinical Disorders, and include the following:

Eating Disorders, Trichotillomania, Body Dysmorphic Disorder, Hypochanondriasis, Paraphilia (preoccupation with sexual urges or fantasies), Substance Use Disorders, Dissociative Disorder, Major Depressive Disorder, Sex and Gender Identiy Disorders, and Schizophrenia.

So do I have OCD? I certainaly have Obsessive/Compulsive tendencies. I've spent eight and ten hour stretches arranging (ordering) things in my apartment. Objects on a coffee table or a dresser "have to" have a certain aesthetic, which depend on the size, shape, and shade of objects and their relationship to each other.

I have another O/C tendency, which I experience as being intrusive. When I can't remember a word, or the title or author of a book or the name of a movie or the actors who starred in it, I can't be at peace until the word, title, or name comes to me, either from my memory or some other source.

But both of my O/C tendencies involve me only occasionally. Neither of them occur with enough frequency to be clinically significant. And the Disorder which I've been enmeshed in for decades, which is clinically significant, can be better explained by one or both of two other Axis 1 Disorders, Body Dysmorphic Disorder and Trichotillomania.

Next I looked up Body Dysmorphic Disorder, which was at one time called Dysmorphobia (fear of ugliness) and at another time calleds Beauty Hypochondria, both of which are more evocative than the current appelation,"Body Dysmorphic Disorder." But what were the diagnostic criteria for BDD, and did I have it?

There are 3 diagnostic criteria listed in DMS 4: (a) preoccupation with an imagined or much exaggerated defect in appearance, (b) which causes clinically significant distress and/or signicicant impairment of social, occupational, (etc.) functioining. (c) The preoccupation isn't better accounted for by another Mental Disorder. Under "associated features" DSM 4 mentions frequent checking of the "defect" in mirrors or other reflecting surfaces, which can consume many hours a day.

DSM 4 also mentions excessive grooming behavior, which may involve things like hair combing, hair removal, ritualized make-up applications, or skin picking.

So do I have Body Dysmorphic Disorder? Yes. I have an overwhelming urge to check flaws in my lashes, hair, or skin. When I check, my perception of my appearance in the mirror is skewed, always on the right side. (I know it's skewed because the right side looks pretty much like the left side in photos.) The incessant attempts to compensate for the flaw(s), (plucking, cutting, breaking of my hair on lashes and/or scalp, repetitive, time consuming application, removal, reapplication and re-removal of make-up), which consume many hours a day are also mentioned in the DSM 4 diagnostic criteria for Body Dysmorphic Disorder. DSM 4 also makes reference to using any available reflecting surface to check flaws and imperfections. It doesn't mention using one's shadow to check and correct, but I'm sure that's an oversight. DSM 4 Also mentions avoidance of mirrors, which was a method I used for curbing my Compulsions after I had been in Cognitive/Behavioral Therapy for a while.

Next I looked up Trichotillomania, which is listed as an Impulse Control Disorder. The diagnostic criteria are: (a) recurrent pulling out of one's hair, resulting in noiceable hair loss, (b) an increasing tension immediately befor pulling or when attempting to resist the behavior, (c) pleasure, gratification, or relief when pulling out hair, (d) the symptoms aren't better accounted for by another mental Disorder or medical condition, and (e) causes clinically significant impairment of social, occupational or other important areas of functiioning.

So do I have Trichotillomania or a checking and grooming, as well as obsessing, variety of Body Dysmorphic Disorder? I believe that I do have Trichotillomania. To begin with, I did pull out lashes. There was a Body Dysmorphic aspect to it, since I didn't get pleasure from pulling out a lash, until I knew it was the "right" lash. If it wasn't I'd have that "oh no!" sensation reminiscent of the first time, when I'd pulled the lashes out accidentally with an eye lash curler. Then I was compelled to keep pulling until I got the "right" hair, which is similar to the "rigid rules" of OCD. The hair cutting, which began in 1986 does have an actual physical pleasure element. I enjoy the sensation of the scissors against my head, cutting off whole sections of hair. Also I have the "can't get my hand out of my hair" Compulsion, which is true of many people with Trichotillomania. In addition, I have frequently found myself breaking hairs unconsciously, before checking to see what damage I've done and/or what hairs still "need" to be broken in the mirror.

It seems to me, after reading the diagnostic criteria for Body Dysmorphic Disorder and Trichotillomania that the two Disorders are intertwined for me, and that the one propels the other.

There was no definition of Obsessive/Compulsive Spectrum Disorder in DSM 4, which surprised me since the term is frequently used by professionals as well as sufferers. In fact, I've been to a conference and a symposium on Obsessive/Compulsive Spectrum Disorders, and the term has always made sense to me.

The Shrouded Women

The shrouded women. I noticed the first, when I was park sitting
with my son Jonathan in '62 or '63. A part of the day that I looked forward to was sitting on a park bench, chatting with the other mothers,
my eyes trained on the sand box, where Jonathan, a sociable toddler,
played amicably–for the most part–with the other children. The day-
time park, with its strange little statue of a peg-legged Peter Stuyvesant,
was clearly segregated. The mommies' and kids' section was in view of
the sandbox, naturally. The old folks sat across from the statue, facing a
fenced in circle of cultivated flowers in the center of the park. There
was a dog run, where dogs and their owners congregated. At the far
end was what I dubbed the pariah section, composed of derelicts and
an assortment of the deranged. A woman, whom I judged to be in her
forties or fifties, who came and sat in this section regularly, completely
concealed her eyes behind huge dark glasses in all seasons and weathers.
And her head, including the hairline, was completely covered by a large
scarf securely knotted under her chin. I remember wondering if she
pulled out her lashes and hair. She seemed totally self-contained and
unapproachable. I could not imagine her communicating with another
human being.

The second shrouded woman was slim and graceful. Her movement
was like that of a soldier trying to avoid enemy fire–or a ghost. I could
not follow her. And I tried, because she fascinated me. As soon as I recognized her, she would be hidden from view by another person, a
truck, a building. She must have turned a corner, but I never actually
saw her do it. Her covering, unlike that of the woman in the park,
went beyond the bounds of social convention; it was bizarre. Not just

her head, but her face, was concealed by a scarf wrapped around several times. There was an eye slit. But that part of her face was hidden behind dark glasses. In addition, she invariably wore long gloves, in any season. In fact, I never really saw any of her surface at all. She made me think of H.G. Wells' *Invisible Man*. Perhaps, I fantasized, it was only her coverings that enabled me to place her in space at all. What seemed more probable was that she was a badly scarred burn victim. Then, one day, after having seen this woman every now and then over a period of several years, I saw her with her face exposed. Neither scarred nor ugly, it was a small soft, rather boneless face, skin pasty from lack of exposure, eyes blinking in the unaccustomed light. I was happy for her–and saddened when I saw her the next time, mummified as before.

I too, have used camouflage: dark glasses, scarves and hats, false eyelashes, wigs, and the cover of night.

Narcissism & Body Dysmorphic Disorder

I once saw an exhibit of small, intense, mesmerizing oil portraits of saints. I identified with Saint Rose of Lima, depicted rubbing a hot pepper into her face, which she did, according to the hand-out, to thwart narcissistic tendencies which arose when someone complimented her on her appearance.

Many, perhaps most, people are dissatisfied with some aspect of their appearance. Ours is a very visual culture, with such a strong link between beauty and sexual desirability that one concept is almost indistinguishable from the other. This has been especially so since the advent of film, with its larger than life images of beauty burned into our brains from an early age. And these screen images create a standard of beauty to which people cannot help but compare themselves. So, naturally, many people are unhappy about their looks. So what's the difference between "normal" dissatisfaction with some aspect of one's face or body and Body Dysmorphic Disorder? One difference is the exaggeration of the defect in BDD. The BDD sufferer has a skewed perception, where the defect or defects are concerned, and such a degree of preoccupation with those defects that he or she may actually be oblivious to obvious defects or serious conditions. Another aspect of BDD is the Compulsion to 'check' the defect and, sometimes, repeated attempts to correct it: a primitive grooming response gone berserk. And this checking, or checking and correcting, may consume most of the sufferer's waking hours.

Primary narcissism: enjoyment of one's own reflection in the glass. Like all pleasures, there's a tendency for it to become an addiction, a need. And like other addictions, indulgence can result in guilt. And for me, the punishment with which I perpetually assuaged the guilt was, conveniently, right there in the glass.

In '73 my apartment was an intense environment in mauve and black. The main living area, two rooms connected by an unobstructed double doorway, was dominated by a long mirror between the two front windows. I was with a lover, in the dining room directly across from the mirror, telling him that our relationship was over. He was angry, wanting me to give the relationship another chance. The odd thing was that instead of looking at him, my gaze was transfixed by my own image, 20 feet away. When he became aware of what I was doing, staring at my reflection, he pointed at the mirror, accusing: "There's your lover." It was true. I was the lover of my reflection, which of course was profoundly frustrating to anyone who was trying to get through to me.

It is odd for me to think of my life in terms of Narcissism/Body Dysmorphic Disorder, because for most of my life I did not recognize the time spent on these related aberrations, the hours spent communing with a mirror instead of with other people or with other aspects of the environment, and the ways in which my relationships, in fact my entire experience, was affected and conditioned by these distortions. There was a split in my consciousness. My ego refused to acknowledge that I was enmeshed in something senseless and out of control, even when the time spent on it included most of my waking hours—and, for most of my life, I had slept little.

I recently had dinner with a friend whose life has been largely devoted to illness. She may or may not be a Hypochondriac, in the sense of imagining illness. But she certainly anticipates illness and is predisposed towards it; there's a strong psychosomatic element. Her relationship to illness is similar to mine with ugliness. She has also been severely depressed for much of the time I've known her, but she recently had a breakthrough. Instead of simply expressing worry and anxiety about her health, she had stepped outside her anxiety and perceived how much of her life these negativities had consumed. She was bitter about the lost years, complaining that life had passed her by, the same sort of regret that people who have been absorbed in Obsessive/ Compulsive Disorder and Obsessive/Compulsive Spectrum Disorders for decades usually experience. In fact, coping with the regret is often the first step in reclaiming one's life. What was so strange was that she used me as the "control subject," contrasting the extent to which her life experience had been circumscribed by self-destructive patterns of thought and behavior, with my life, which she perceived as being rich in variety and drama. Certainly, I had involved myself in drama and forced drastic (frequently destructive) change in order to avoid the reality that I spent most of my time enslaved by repetitive Obsession and Compulsion. Then, when I was 'free,' I ignored that time and focused on the narrative of what I did during the brief periods in between, attempting to mentally compensate for the endless hours when my horizon extended no farther than my eyelashes–literally.

Europe—'76, '77

My health had begun to break down on the train to Paris, although I had felt fine before leaving New York. It was several months before I discovered the cause of the flu-like symptoms that I was experiencing such as respiratory discomfort, low-grade fever, and muscle soreness. One day, for no apparent reason, my stomach blew up, making it appear that I was about six months pregnant. I also had severe cramps. These new symptoms worried me enough to send me to a hospital, where I learned that my symptoms had been caused by an IUD, which had moved, causing an infection in the fallopian tubes, which had spread throughout my body. The IUD was surgically removed, and I was given massive doses of antibiotics, first for nine days by IV in the hospital, and then for two weeks by injection, during daily visits to an out-patient clinic. My recovery was slow. My illness served to focus my attention on the functioning of my body, rather than on my appearance. My Dysmorphic Obsessions and Compulsions receded for a time.

In the spring of '77, my Paris roommate, Claire, and I visited Amsterdam. In contrast with Paris (or New York), the ambience of Amsterdam was free and natural. And I felt more comfortable with my appearance, because a sizable portion of the population has my sort of coloring–invisibly pale lashes and brows. So I didn't need to camouflage the paleness with cosmetics. I stopped tweezing out 'wrong' lashes and substituted cutting them with a nail scissors, which felt less drastic. And I was no longer spending frustrating hours alternating sticking the lashes together with mascara and rubbing my lid raw, wiping the mascara off. I felt as if I had removed a mask. I continued to have bouts of resperatory illness, which were probably a continuation of the systemic illness caused originally by the IUD.

In June Claire went off to India and I to Greece. On the Isle of Crete, I had a dreadful respiratory episode. I lay on a beach for two and a half days, gasping for air, feeling caught between life and death, praying for release into one or the other. I recovered completely, and, in fact, felt very strong. I swam and climbed and rode a motor bike around the island. But I became ill again a month and a half later, on an island off the coast of Denmark. It was very cold at night even though it was summer. I suffered in the freezing night air and was unable to sleep. It was clear to me that I needed warmth, which was why, when my friend Maryanne asked me to join her in Hawaii, I knew it was just what I needed.

Hawaii—'77–'80

I was in Hawaii for two and a half years. Most of my time there was spent out of doors, without an easily accessible mirror. My life involved much more physical exertion than it had for many years, with regular swimming, climbing, and outdoor cooking, that began with gathering branches to make the fire. I became involved with various spiritual groups, and began to meditate. All of these factors combined to loosen the bond of my Dysmorphic Obsession and its attendant Compulsions. The environment produced a high degree of behavior modification without effort and, unfortunately, without awareness. So from the time I returned to New York in the summer of 1980, the Disorder became gradually, insidiously, more pervasive. I again became dissatisfied with the paleness of my lashes, the lack of definition. I began to use a kohl pencil, which darkened the base of both upper and lower lashes. The mask was back, and I was again spending hours creating it. I had the sensation that the pressure of the pencil on the underside of my lid encouraged lashes to grow in the bare stretches of the upper right lid, and I was still cutting, sometimes perilously close to the lids.

Secondary Gains

I had returned to New York with a man I'd been living with in Hawaii. We lived in a variety of hotel rooms and apartments in New York, always in very tight quarters, in painfully close proximity to each other. Ron's presence served to curtail my Compulsions—out of the need to maintain secrecy. But with or without a roommate, my Compulsions were always particularly intractable when anticipation of an emotionally fraught event caused my anxiety to rise. I missed my grandfather's funeral because of my Disorder. I've always regretted that I couldn't be there, but the mirror held me transfixed. I couldn't resist its magnetic pull. Then, shortly after I returned to New York, my cousin Gloria died. Gloria was young and vivacious, and her death was wrenching. But as desperately as I wanted to attend her funeral, I was unable to be there. I was full of remorse over my failure to show up. Were regret and remorse the 'real' payoff? Most of the time, I arrived late at wherever I was supposed to be. My inability to be punctual, to be in control of when or even whether I would be able to be some place, produced both self-loathing and resentment against whomever was disappointed or inconvenienced because of my absence or lateness—whomever my inadequacy had been revealed to.

Contempt, loathing, and self-condemnation was always what I experienced after a long period submerged in Body Dysmorphic/Trichotillomaniac Obsessions and Compulsions. The time spent lost in Compulsions had diminished considerably. But now I felt that since I knew what was going on, I should be able to completely refrain from indulging in Body Dysmorphic/Trichotillomaniac Obsessions and Compulsions. Of course, relapse into BDD isn't the only kind of failure that I condemn myself for. Self-condemnation is itself a tendency. One way of perceiving the chain of events is that I perpetuate the Disorder precisely because it's a sure-fire way to perpetuate a condemnatory attitude toward myself. This doesn't mean that episodes of capitulation to Obsessions and Compulsions begin with self-loathing. Usually, they begin with being stymied with respect to some decision: Is there time to bathe now, or should I get dressed and leave, and bathe after I return? I seem to have a deeply ingrained notion that everything should be resolved, or at least obvious, and that I shouldn't have to use my mind to search out solutions. My mind wants to just roll on unimpeded. I'm not one of those people who resents having her sleep disturbed–I can usually go back to sleep if I so desire. It's when I'm awake that I don't want to be bothered. That's why having a friend stay with me for three months during the fall of '96 was a challenge and an opportunity to explore my assumption that if someone else were there, it would more difficult to function. I always expect that it will be difficult to think if I'm being continually deluged with someone else's observations and assertions. It's odd, because I've always known that spending relatively circumscribed periods of time in company was mentally stimulating, in fact essential to productive thought. What happens when I lapse into OC symptoms? I'm experiencing an inner struggle between the possibility of interaction with people or even representations such as books, tapes, and videos, and living purely in my own mind, being the sole creator, perceiver, knower. It seems to me that there is something in this defense against outside influence and input, encroachment, against giving attention to anything or anyone, which resembles Autism. In fact, when I read Donna Williams' book, *Nobody Nowhere,* I found that in many respects I identified with her experience of being Autistic. But in that continuum from involuntary to voluntary, my refusal to interact has a great enough element of choice that I feel guilty about not doing so. Being stuck, creating ugliness, etc. is a punishment for refusing to be impinged on by others. I have been my own jailer. Paradoxically, when I was in jail for four days in the summer of '71, because the car I had purchased on the street and negrlected to register turned out to be stolen, I was temporarily liberated from both my Disorder and my addiction to cigarettes.

The Elephant Woman

I saw her on the number 2 train, when I boarded at 14th Street. I spotted her sitting across from me, as I leaned against the far door.

She was young and slim and Black, but with a malformation so extreme that none of those categories seemed relevant, not even gender. Large irregular folds of skin hung down from her chin and jaws to the level of her shoulders, completely obscuring her throat and neck. Looking at her made my throat muscles contract and my eyes sting.

"The poor unfortunate woman," I thought. "If her affliction were mine, it would drive me insane." Then I saw the person behind the freak. She was sane, and was not full of bitterness or self-pity.

I was once close to suicide because some of my hair fell out, following the birth of my first child. What a high value I put on my life!

My attention was again drawn to the Elephant Woman as she rose from her seat. When she alighted from the train, all I saw was her slim back, her graceful limbs, and her shoulder-length black hair.

BDD Concerns Obscure More Or Less Serious Physical Conditions

When I first heard that people with BDD can be so immersed in a specific imagined or exaggerated ugliness that they ignore real deformity or disability, I said gaily, "so maybe I'm a hunchbacked dwarf, and completely unaware of it." In reality, the condition I ignored was that my pallet bone was shrinking, my gums deteriorating, my teeth becoming progressively looser, falling out, one by one, over a period of a decade, a condition caused by a combination of bad genes and iron implants (implants should by made of titanium), which had been inserted by a nut named Dr. Linkow, and by my not focusing on the problem except when I was in serious pain. I now have implants and a dental prosthesis.

Diary Selections 1995

10/10/95   Today I decided to organize the material for this book. Good idea. I had dental implants inserted in my gum two days ago, and my face has all these unanticipated, evolving mountains and valleys: a whole new landscape every time I look in the mirror. My decision to organize my material has prevented me from becoming totally immersed in the fascinating, but fortunately temporary, horrors of my physiognomy.

Unfortunately, I ended up going into a tailspin over what was missing from the two drawers of materials relating to my book. I didn't have a record of the first letter I'd sent to Christina Dubowsky, founder of the Tricotillomania Learning Center, because it was on the first (stolen) computer. My obsessive need to have a particular piece of information was almost assuaged when I came across a hand-written note from her. It said: "Dear Jenifer,—I too, know what it's like to be a prisoner in my own body! Here's our basic info pack. I hope it helps. You are not alone.—Love, Christina."

Then I didn't have the last note I'd written to Dr. Phillips. That's because it was on a Season's Greetings card. The essence of my note was that I'd reached a dead end. What more did I need to know about it?

That Obsessive/Compulsive "need" to have some particular piece of information: how does it differ from how most people perceive the need for a specific bit of information, and how they go about obtaining it? Actually, I hadn't been aware that my inability to accept frustration in attempting to obtain specific information was in any way abnormal, until someone at a support group spoke of his exaggerated willingness to spend any amount of time and go to any lengths to obtain some "absolutely essential" bit of data. And the importance of the information, the frantic intensity of the desire for it increases in direct relation to the difficulty of procuring it. Always, in retrospect, he can see (if he was successful in his quest) that the bit of information wasn't really all that crucial. If he failed to find what he was looking for (even if it was years ago) he knows intellectually that it wouldn't have transformed his life; yet, he doesn't totally accept it. Yes. That is my experience. The information may become intensely important, almost solely because it is missing, or feared to be missing. And, for me, not only is it missing *information*, which can set off a frantic quest, it can be a missing garment, a lost piece of jewelry, a decorative object, or one fraught with sentiment. Or it may be something that combines information and object, like a book or a piece of paper. The painful sensation I experience when engaged in one of these anxious searches is almost identical to what I feel while desperately trying to get my hair "right."

10/18/95   Damn! I've lost another night to it. Both my hair and lashes seem all right now; but it's 4 am and I have to wake up in three hours.

When I'm lost in it, the passage of time means nothing: all I want is for my hair/lashes to look OK to me. I regret the lost time only after the Disorder has released me and I can walk away from the mirror. My regret is that, once again, I have stifled growth and evolution. *Mirror, Mirror, on the wall, I'm sick and tired of You!*

10/25/95   I went to see Dr. Laakso again, having decided to take another stab at using a Specific Serotonin Reuptake Inhibitor antidepressant. Her price had jumped from $50 for 15 minutes to $85 for fifteen minutes. And at least five minutes were spent in her urging me to get health insurance, so I could have longer sessions. In fact, this time around, all I'd come for was a prescription. I figured a month's worth would give me a good idea of whether or not to continue on it. I mean, I know that much of the OCD literature says that an antidepressant may take two or three months to kick in for some Obsessive/Compulsive patients. I don't disagree with that; but I'm not willing to put something that toxic into my body for that long without seeing some dramatic results.

In any case, she wasn't about to give me the opportunity to really try the drug for a mere $85. Instead of giving me a prescription, she gave me a sample of Wellbutrin (bupropion), a week's supply. At the end of the week I felt that there had been a slight change. It seemed to me that I spent less time Obsesssing and Compulsing in front of a mirror, and more time productively or pleasurably engaged. I had made an appointment for two weeks after the initial visit, because I had thought there were more pills than there actually were. I felt resentful, and decided not to invest any more time, money, energy on trying for a pharmaceutical cure through Dr. Laakso. I called to cancel. I was angry when I received her bill for a "phone session," which had lasted about five minutes. But once I was over the initial outrage, I realized that it didn't matter if the session was in person or over the phone, two minutes or twenty. What I had expected from the initial visit was a prescription. I called Dr. Laakso and said that if she called a prescription in to my pharmacy, I'd pay the bill. And that's what happened. I felt good that I'd turned a lose/lose into a win/win—or so I thought. As for the Wellbutrin, I couldn't really get a handle on whether or not it was helping significantly. That, combined with its unpleasantly, toxicly edgy feel made me decide to discontinue it after a month. Most of the literature says that Obsessive/Compulsive Disorder is significantly ameliorated through the use of Selective Serotonin Re-uptake Inhibitors in about 60% of patients who try them. So far, I'm in the other 40%. What I didn't realize then was that Wellbutrin is not a Selective Serotonin Re-uptake Inhibitor. Rather it is a unique drug which works on two brain chemicals: norepinephrine and dopamine, but **not** on serotonin, which is the brain chemical usually considered critical in

OCD and OCSDs. If only I'd known! But since I assumed that Well-butrin was an SSRI rcommended for OCSDs, I thought that SSRIs didn't work for me and that I had no choice but to use my mind to combat my mental Disorder, which is the essence of Cognitive Therapy. The core of Cognitive Therapy is changing your thinking patterns in such a way that you become aware that the problem isn't as it appears. In other words, as soon as I begin checking my hair, I need to switch into "I don't have a hair problem, I have a brain chemistry problem, which won't be improved by spending the next three hours attempting to fix my hair." This requires that I relinquish instinct and intuition, the inner voices that normally guide us through life, in favor of what I know with the mind only.

AMI/FAMI OCD Meeting

I attended a once-a-month OCD support group meeting at AMI/FAMI (acronyms for Alliance of the Mentally Ill, and Family and Advocates for the Mentally Ill). For the most part, the organization is concerned with Schizophrenias and Bi-polar Disorder. The reason the OCD meeting was held there was because the organizer, Norman Levy, had a connection with the organization. Mr. Levy also wrote about mental illness. He was sensitive and supportive, a good person to chair a meeting.

This was not a 12-step meeting but formatted instead on the 'Consciousness Raising' model, which includes dialogue, relevant conversation, after each participant makes her or his initial presentation.

When it was my turn, I said that I had Trichotilomania, an unusual cutting variety connected with Body Dysmorphic Obsessions. The cutting had stopped over the past couple of weeks. I added that, unfortunately, I seemed to have exchanged the cutting Compulsion for breaking hair in an ineffectual effort to even it out. I was caught in a repetitive cycle: a short remission followed by my breaking hairs, first an occasional hair, then breaking hair continuously, finally a resumption of cutting when the breaking had made my hair hopelessly uneven, which ultimately led to baldness as I pressed the scissors closer and closer to the scalp.

Someone suggested that I have my hair professionally cut. He analogized having someone cut my hair to the kind of "flooding" done in contamination OCD, where the person forces her/himself to do that which is particularly abhorrent and discovers that it doesn't lead to death and destruction. As an example, he said that a therapist might advise a patient with contamination OCD to touch the bottom of his shoe, and not wash his hands for half an hour.

I said I wasn't afraid to cut my hair. On the contrary, once I started, I couldn't stop. My fear wasn't of cutting, but of not being able to stop myself from cutting until I'd made myself bald, because I've done it so many times. I said that Tricotilomania was an impulse control Disorder, which in some respects was like an addiction: the only way to stop is to stop. And I was terrified that I'd never be able to stop

A few days later, when I had a desperate urge to cut my hair, I decided that in spite of logical considerations and in spite of the fact that professional cuts in the past had not even slowed down my own cutting, to follow the advice I'd been given in the group and have my hair cut professionally. The cut, as usual, was not completely satisfactory. So on each of the next three days, I spent about 15 minutes a day doing remedial cutting. I was not surprised that the professional cut had precipitated some additional cutting. To the contrary, I felt fortunate that the professional cut hadn't resulted in a full-scale relapse.

Tricotillomania Conference In New York

I looked forward to the Trichotillomania conference, hoping for new insight. This conference, held in a church in Greenwich Village, was like a very large support group meeting. I enjoyed both sharing and listening to others share in this relaxed, almost festive atmosphere.

The most engaging speaker was a 12-year-old boy who spoke about his hair pulling, as well as examining the roots in minute detail. He was with his parents, who had obviously empowered him. He was squeezing his "behavior mod" balls, as he spoke. His openness and objectivity, and the effort he made were inspiring.

Naomi Sarna, who runs Trichotillomania group therapy sessions, said that people put themselves into a trance state during the pulling process, almost a meditation. True, there is a one pointedness about pulling, or, in my case, cutting; but, unlike the results of meditation, increased energy and alertness, the results of Tric trance for me are despondency and demoralization. Ms. Sarna also said that people with Trichotillomania are unusually tactile: they're always stroking things, like fabrics, because they enjoy the feel of various textures. That's why the Behavior Modification techniques for Trichotillomania always involve keeping the hands busy. I noticed that Ms. Sarna's statement, that Trichotillomaniacs were exceptionally tactile, was affirmed by most of the participants. It doesn't apply to me. I sometimes want to stroke a person or an animal to show affection, but I have little desire to rub things to feel their texture. It's my visual sense that always needs to be engaged. I do use my hands a lot, but not because I enjoy touching things. I don't touch things. Rather, I take hold of them when I want to change them, to make them more pleasing to myself, functionally or aesthetically. And that kind of activity, fixing, rearranging, occasionally making objects, can become as compulsive as cutting, breaking, or rearranging hair. In other words, my hands do have to be engaged, but, more frequently than not, in conjunction with my eyes. I exchanged phone numbers with a few women before I left.

Christina Dubowsky On Support Groups

In April of 1996 I went to a symposium on Obsessive/Compulsive Spectrum Disorders, wondering if anyone had come up with any new ideas about either of the two I've been enmeshed in.

It was the second time I'd heard Christina Dubowsky, founder and prime mover of the Trichotillomania Learning Center. She gave a workshop on forming and maintaining support groups. I told her that I wanted to organize a support group for people with OC Spectrum Disorders, since I have at least two of them: Body Dysmorphic Disorder and Trichotillomania. Actually, I hadn't realized I wanted to form a support group until I heard myself say so. Christina suggestested that I limit the group to people with body-focused Disorders, which seemed just right, and offered to mail me a brochure pertaining to initiating and facilitating a support group. I eagerly accepted.

The brochure was neatly divided. The first page gave advice on how to organize a group: networking and advertising. It discussed alternatives for where and when to hold meetings, and phone accessibility. The page ended with the caution that support groups tend to develop slowly, so persistence is necessary. The second page was composed of two paragraphs. The first was concerned with the purpose of a support group, powerfully stated in the last sentence: "This is a safe and non-judgmental place in which to explore and heal, and one of the major goals of the group is to assist each individual in moving beyond compulsive behavior, when they are ready." The second paragraph described the format that Christina used. It began with each person sharing for three to five minutes, uninterruptedly. After that, the group should be open to discussion. Within the discussion framework, she cautioned, support, not confrontation, should be the goal. This was precisely the format I remembered being used in Consciousness Raising groups in the early '70s, a format which still appealed to me. Christina also sent me her list of people in the New York area, possible recruits for a support group. I was elated.

Soon after that, I received a letter from a group that called itself "The New York Tricotillomania Learning Center Organizing Committee," asking me to come to an organizing meeting, the result of having given my number to someone at the Tricotillomania conference at the Church. I was confused. Should I join their group, and perhaps facilitate a group under their auspices? Or should I simply try to get a group going? The problem, for me, was that, although Christina had told me she had expanded her groups to include people with other body-focused Disorders, the conference out of which this group had blossomed was solely concerned with Trichotillomania. I decided to attend the meeting anyway.

Dreams As Guides

In the process of making decisions, dreams can offer guidance through revealing what one really hopes to gain—or fears to lose. And it disturbed me that I was rarely able to remember my dreams, in spite of having made efforts to do so. Therefore, I felt very fortunate when I remembered my dreams two days in a row.

In the first dream, I found myself in front of a health food restaurant, mesmerized by an appetizing assortment of take-out goodies. I didn't recognize the shop, nor did I recognize my behavior with respect to it. In real life, it has never been difficult for me to resist expensive and unnecessary food. But in the dream, I entered the store and bought $13 worth of luxury food, baked goods, jams and nectars. I showed my friend Gloria what I'd bought. Then, realizing that I needed a heavy-duty shopping bag to shlep it all home comfortably, I ran into the store, leaving my bag on the pavement, expecting Gloria to watch it. (I dreamt this dream during a two-hour nap, after which I expected to meet Gloria for dinner, so it's not surprising that she was in the dream.) Out on the sidewalk again with my shopping bag, I discovered that both Gloria and my goodies were gone. Then Gloria emerged from the store with her own bag of stuff. Mine, neglected, had been stolen.

When I related the dream to Gloria, her interpretation was that I was feeling neglected by my friends. I didn't disagree, but I felt there was something else, that the uncharacteristic food-buying binge and the theft were important elements too. My mother always told me that I didn't want much, which was never the case. The truth is that I've always assumed I wouldn't be able to get what I wanted, or that it would be taken away from me before I could enjoy it. And of course, these assumptions became self-fulfilling prophesies.

The second dream that I remembered also took place during an afternoon nap. It seemed to refer back to the Trichotillomania organization meeting two days earlier. The dream took place in "my apartment," which looked neither like my real apartment, nor like the apartment in which the actual meeting had been held.

In the dream, everyone was seated around a long table. I, alone, didn't have a seat at the table, nor could I understand what was being discussed. And no one would answer my questions. I was outraged. How dare they ostracize me in my own place! They had brought food to munch on during a break. While their mouths were full, I began to yell at them.

"Who do you think you are," I screamed, "excluding and ignoring me? Get the hell out of here." Moving with great speed, I threw their food on the floor, something my younger son did when he was in day care at too early an age. Is that what I feel like, as powerless as a one-year old? I'm an angry little match girl, left out in the cold, excluded from the feast of life.

The dream did bear more than a passing resemblance to the actual Trichotillomania Learning Center organizing meeting. The three "official" TLC women were rather cliquish and exclusionary. When there was a discussion about forming support groups, I said that I would like to include people with other Body Focused Disorders, because I think there's a common thread, both physiologically and psychologically. Not responding, they were focused and incurious and apparently felt I was wasting time. They wanted to talk only about networking and organizing. Their desire was to educate the world about Trichotillomania, rather than to discuss their own thoughts and feelings about it. In spite of my dissatisfaction with the organizing meeting, I hadn't been able to decide whether to keep on attending their meetings, or to try forming a group of my own. The dream helped me decide: I was going to have to overcome my natural inertia and do some networking. I subsequently learned from Christina Dubowsky that the connection of the Organizing Committee with the Trichotillomania Learning Center was no more "official" than mine, that TLC had no chapters in New York or anywhere else.

Organizing A Support Group

Using the list of New York area TLC contacts that Christina had sent, I called people who hadn't been at the organizing meeting. This process netted two possibilities, neither of whom (as it turned out) actually came to a meeting. But I was able to help one of them find a treatment provider in her area, from the list of treatment providers I had received from the Obsessive/Compulsive Foundation.

Next, I sent a letter to 60 of the clinicians: psychiatrists and psychologists, as well as directors of Anxiety Disorders clinics, who were on the O/CF list. I included two copies of a flier, announcing the support group which could be given to patients. It said:

Announcing A New Peer Support Group...for people with body-focused Obsessions and/or Compulsions, including, but not limited to: Dysmorphic Disorder, Hypochondria, Trichotillomania, Self-Mutilation, Anorexia, Bulimia, Tics.

When I went to have copies of my flier made, the woman working in the copy shop said that her roommate had one of the Disorders mentioned in my flier. She evidently felt the condition too shameful to call by name, but my sense of it was that she had bulimia. I gave her a flier and encouraged her to have her roommate get in touch with me.

Then, in the post office, while I was putting fliers and letters to psychiatrists and psychologists into manila envelopes, a man across the table from me was making barking sounds and doing something strange with his arms, both of which distracted my attention. I couldn't keep track of which pile of envelops had been stuffed and which hadn't. I was enraged at the man, until I realized that he had

Tourette Syndrome, and that I, who had had Tourette Syndrome as a child, still had it on occasion, should be tolerant of his uncontrollable sounds and movements. I can still hear my father angrily hissing "stop it!" when the muscles in my jaw and neck twitched uncontrollably, unbearably, and when the need to clear my throat every few seconds was irresistible.

Symposium On Obsessive/ Compulsive Spectrum Disorders

In July of '96, I attended a symposium on Obsessive/Compulsive Spectrum Disorders organized by Eric Hollander, Director of the Anxiety Disorders Clinic at Mount Sinai Hospital (whose article on the same subject I had copied for my group) and Jim Broatch, Director of the Obsessive/Compulsive Foundation. I had been to a symposium on OCD, and another on Trichotillomania. This was the second time I was going to a symposium about the gamut of interrelated Disorders that I've suffered from–Body Dysmorphic Disorder, Tics, Trichotillomania, and (briefly) Self-mutilation and Depersonalization Disorder. I hoped there would be some exploration of the way in which people shift from one Disorder to another. My own perception is that I've moved from one *manifestation* of the Disorder to another. That is, I see Tics, Trichotillomania, etc. as being different manifestations of the same Disorder.

The first thing I heard was that with treatments now in use, 50% of sufferers have 70% or better reduction of symptoms. Not great, but certainly better than nothing. Dr. Hollander spoke of a reduction of symptoms rather than of a cure, which has certainly been my experience. He also talked about the drugs now in use, the Selective Serotonin Re-uptake Inhibitors, like Luvox (fluvoxamine), Prozac (fluoxetine), Paxil (paroxetine), and Zoloft (sertraline), which, he said, help to put patients "back in the driver's seat" in their lives.

Dr. Hollander said that, on average, patients suffer for seven or eight years before revealing their Disorder, and another seven years before finding appropriate treatment. Knowing what the problem is and what resources are available to ameliorate it is crucial. In that sense, the news is good, since both the Spectrum of Disorders and treatments for them are becoming more widely known.

Dr. Hollander enumerated the various Obsessive/Compulsive Spectrum Disorders: Somataform (body-focused) Disorders, such as Body Dysmorphic Disorder and Anorexia; Dissociative Disorder, in which the sufferer has a sense of unreality, either about herself or others; and Impulse Control Disorders, including Trichotillomania, Compulsive Masturbation, and Compulsive Gambling. Dr. Hollander linked this wide range of Disorders through the fact that all of them have responded to the Selective Serotonin Re-uptake Inhibitors. He said the professionals in the field were hoping for further confirmation of the linkage through MRI imaging looking at different regions of the brain. He also said that the tendency for the brain to make inadequate use of Serotonin was hereditary, and that this tendency was frequently exacerbated by pregnancy. I found the last idea interesting, because it was during my first pregnancy that I had my first and only episode of Dissociative Disorder.

Among the statistics offered by Dr. Hollander was that 40% of patients with Obsessive/Compulsive and Obsessive/Compulsive Spectrum Disorders can't work for long periods of time. This can occur, he said, because it's so difficult to break away from Obsessive/Compulsive rituals long enough to leave the house. He also said that there are other sufferers for whom the work environment simply provides a new venue for Obsessions and Compulsions to manifest and multiply, making it impossible to do a satisfactory job. And, whether at home or at work, it may be impossible for such individuals to separate legitimate concerns and the actions necessary to deal with them from Obsessive concerns and the rituals performed to assuage them.

Norman Levy, the master of ceremonies at the symposium, was a benign presence here, as he'd been as chairman of the AMI/FAMI OCD support group. He talked about his own experience, some of which I'd heard before. His symptoms began when he was an officer of his Tenants' Association. As part of his duties, he examined the physical structure of his building and became afraid that the building, or parts of it, would collapse. Ultimately, he became obsessed with these fears and was compelled to do a lot of checking in hopes of assuaging them. He said that he had had a substantial recovery, which he attributed largely to a fine-tuning of drugs. As he spoke I thought about a building on Thirteenth Street, where the lintel over the front door became dislodged, killing one girl and paralyzing another. I wondered how he would have reacted to this event. I mean, the premise of Behavior Modification Therapy with respect to Obsessive/Compulsive Disorder, and several of the Obsessive/Compulsive Spectrum Disorders, is the concept that we must live with uncertainty. An occurrence like the one just mentioned can happen, but very rarely happens, so it doesn't make sense to spend one's life worrying that it might.

Jim Broatch spoke about the fact that Behavior Therapy can work alone, without the deleterious side effects frequently experienced with drugs. He said that only four out of ten sufferers exposed themselves to Behavior Modification Therapy. The Behavioral techniques commonly take the form of delaying a Compulsive ritual. For me, it has translated into covering the bathroom mirror and ridding my apartment of scissors and razors. The concept is that if you refrain from performing the rituals for longer and longer periods of time, they gradually diminish in frequency and duration, while Obsessions become both less intense and less pervasive.

Gearing Up For My Group

I learned that Jim Broatch had put my name and number in the O/C Foundation newsletter, when I began to receive calls from people who had seen it there. Some were interested in my projected support group, while others simply wanted to discuss their symptoms and struggles. Some were calling about family members, who were too diffident to call themselves. In the last category was a woman calling about her son, who she said had Obsessions related to his appearance, along with Compulsive rituals carried out in the bathroom. I gathered that the son was at home, and wondered if he was a child. When I inquired, the mother said no, he was 25. The reason she was calling at this juncture was because he planned to move to his own apartment, and she was afraid that he would become overwhelmed away from home, a not unreasonable fear. I spoke with her twice, feeling that it was a pity that the son didn't call, since transcending fear, shame, and other obstructive emotions enough to seek support for your recovery is valuable in itself, even if you don't find what you're looking for on the first try.

One woman who called was interested in a support group but lived too far from Manhattan to consider becoming a member of the one I was attempting to form. Her immediate need was for receptivity and validation. She had participated in a short in-patient substance abuse program, and now, after her release from the hospital, was spending most of her time in therapy and in therapist-led support groups, which all concerned substance abuse. She was not getting either support or therapy for her Trichotillomania, because such support was not available in the relatively rural area in which she lived. We spoke for a couple of hours. I gave her the address and number of the Trichotillomania Learning Center and encouraged her to contact them. She sounded less anxious at the end of our conversation than she had at the beginning.

A woman I'd given my number to at the TLC conference at the church called. She was extremely disturbed and needed to ventilate. Sandra was twentysomething and very much involved in anger at her parents, holding them responsible for her Disorder even though she understood intellectually that brain chemistry plays a decisive role in Tricholtillomania. She had begun pulling out her lashes and brows when she was an adolescent at boarding school, as I had in summer camp at the same age. Trichotillomania frequently has its onset in adolescence which, for most people is a time of high anxiety in any case. And the fears about approaching adulthood were exacerbated for Sandra, as they were for me, by being away from home. Now that she was in New York on her own, instead of being able to enjoy her freedom, as she'd anticipated, she was more intensely consumed by her Disorder than ever and felt ugly, miserable, and full of self-loathing, very much as I had during my first year at the University of Chicago so many years ago. I tried to get her to see how fortunate she was to be a young adult now, when much is known about treating her Disorder. She wasn't interested in a support group.

Finally, two people who said they were interested in a support group called, but neither of them came to the meeting we'd arranged. In a way, it was a relief. I'd worked hard on making my apartment presentable. I began with cleaning but ended spending endless hours rearranging furniture and a variety of small decorative objects, such as crystals, candles, candy dishes, ash trays, and sculpture, but hadn't made copies of articles for discussion. There were two that I had in mind: Dr. Hollander's overview of Obsessive/Compulsive Spectrum Disorders, because it provided a rationale for organizing a group around Body-Focused Obsessive/Compulsive Spectrum Disorders; and a New York Times piece, by Daniel Goleman, on achieving the same changes in brain function with Behavior Mod techniques as with meds, which would provide a basis for discussing what we've experienced with one and/or the other of these treatments.

More important than cleaning and arranging my space or even making copies of the two articles, which I rather expected people to read at home for discussion at the second meeting, was psyching myself, which involved thinking about time (format) rather than space. There was an analogy here with a weekly dance class I once gave. When I taught dance, I liked to work extemporaneously, but without fear of drawing a blank. What I did was to write a list of exercises that I could refer to if it became necessary. What I needed was a plan for the first meeting, even though much of the meeting would probably be taken up with getting acquainted. I wrote down a list of possible topics for discussion:

1. Grooming activities—How are they employed to relieve anxiety? How are they used to avoid decision making?

2. Hypnotherapy—How is it used in the treatment of Obsessive/ Compulsive Spectrum Disorders?

3. Behavior Modification Therapy—How do therapists use it in the treatment of OCSDs? What about self-initiated Behavior Modification exercises?

4. Pharmacology—How useful are SSRIs in the treatment of Obsessive/Compulsive Spectrum Disorders?

5. How are Biofeedback techniques (and technology) used in the treatment of OCSDs?

6. How might Yoga, especially Pranayama (breath control), help to relieve symptoms of OCSDs? How about Meditation? Afirmations?

7. Exercise: Visualize yourself living through a day or an evening free from symptoms. How would it be more pleasurable? In what respects would it be more difficult?

Relapse Again

I didn't recognize the relapse until it was well under way. Each day for at least two weeks, I'd been spending progressively more time rearranging my hair, taking a cut here and there, breaking a few hairs a day. Then one day, I cut off all of the hair in the back. Oddly, I'd done it so that if I looked into the mirror head on, I couldn't see what I'd done; but everyone else could. So there it was: I had relapsed. What had caused the Obsessions and Compulsions to gain momentum? Obviously, high anxiety, caused by not having a job, and knowing that my unemployment insurance would soon run out. When I looked at the New York Times want ads, all it did was increase my anxiety, focusing on all of the jobs I'm not qualified for. The day I cut off all the hair in back, I was preparing to go to my grandson's first birthday party. My mother and my two sons would be there, so I anticipated that caught-between-the-generations-everyone-judging-me-and-finding-me-wanting feeling. I dealt with the anticipated discomfort through the simple expedient of bringing a camera, which enables me to think of myself as an observer, rather than an object of observation (and judgment). And I realized I would be playing with a one year old and a two-and-a-half year old, which can be totally absorbing. Why couldn't I have thought of those things before I'd made myself look unacceptable? There had been other times during my nine-month semi-remission when I'd been worried about money and apprehensive in anticipation of a family gathering. The novel factor, the one I believe made a relapse all but inevitable, was that I had sufficient confidence in my level of recovery to feel that I could help others, to organize and facilitate a support group. And, in one fell swoop, I'd demolished my credibility—or at least I felt that I had.

My Support Group

There were three of us, Cindy, Doreen and I. The first meeting was at Doreen's apartment, the apartment she'd lived in with her recently divorced husband. Doreen had been diagnosed with Body Dysmorphic Disorder, whose onset had been less than a year earlier, not much after her divorce. Clearly, she felt that life wasn't treating her fairly. She didn't want to return to her marriage but was annoyed that her ex seemed to be fairing better than she. She had been a model—her face and figure were lovely—but said that recently she hadn't been able to get modeling work and had been forced to take a boring and poorly paid clerical job, which she found demeaning. She felt that if she could get a face lift which would restore her former beauty, all of her problems would go away. Unfortunately, she couldn't afford plastic surgery. What she said seemed to deny her diagnosis. So why was she in Cognitive/Behavioral Therapy and why had she chosen to be in a support group for people with body focused Disorders? She must have known, at least part of the time, that she had an Obsessional Disorder. But during our meeting she apparantly had no doubt that her skewed perceptions were correct. She showed Cindy and me professional photos taken ten years earlier, and while it was true that her face had changed, she was still gorgeous. It was the intensity of her focus on the changes in her face that convinced me that she had Body Dysmorphic Disorder. Also, the spoke about having had an acting career, which she assumed was over because of the change in her appearance. This obviously didn't make sense. If her acting career was over it was because she'd given up on it.

The second meeting was at Cindy's and the focus was on her. Cindy said that her Trichotillomania had begun two years earlier, after she'd been raped. It was a college "date rape," so she knew her assailant. She'd tried to have him expelled, to no avail. So he'd gotten away with it, which increased her sense of victimization. Working in a rape crises center had given her some sense of vindication. But the rape and its unsatisfactory aftermath were still very much with her. She was fragile, but coping, and very sensitive to other people's problems. I'm sure the women who encountered her in the rape crises center appreciated her.

When I got home from my grandson's birthday party at about 9:30 at night I spoke with both Cindy and Doreen, the two women who'd been to the first two meetings. This was the first time I was able to do what they tell you to do at Obsessive Compulsive Anonymous meetings—call someone in the group, in order to defuse anxiety, get a fresh perspective, and avoid lapsing into the Obsessive/Compulsive cycle. Cindy, who had Trichotillomania, said she'd felt thwarted all day, lonely and depressed, because a plan with a friend had fallen through. She'd forced herself to go to two museums, so she wouldn't wallow. It was good for me to hear loneliness expressed, because I rarely recognize my own as such: it feels too shameful.

Then Doreen called, echoing my discomfort with the signs of aging in my face. In my attempt to help her to distinguish legitimate concerns from Dysmorphic Obsessiveness, I helped myself to sort it out—for the time being.

Doreen's Obsessive concern, which she said had begun a year earlier, was a fullness around the jaw that hadn't been there before. My Obsessive face concern was a wattle under my chin. We both felt the offensive changes kinetically, as well as seeing them reflected in the mirror, the evidence of one sense confirming the evidence of the other. And for both of us, either sense could be the first "spike."

My (hair cutting) relapse continued, so discouraging after months of thinking that the demands of my Disorder were now manageable.

Finally, the anxiety related to the immanent need to find work broke through the surface numbness. That is, it became a conscious and constant worry. I realized that I had made finding work really impossible by reversing day and night in terms of being awake and asleep.

I spent three hours pushing my lashes around with tweezers and a lash/brow brush, checking, checking, checking, finding the flaw, zeroing in on it, fixing it, creating more flaws, and on and on. Then hair: arranging and disarranging, over and over. I could see that I'd created a high level of tension by pressuring myself to reach out. I didn't want to go to work or have meetings. I just wanted to disappear.

I was Gulliver examining the face of a Brobdingnag. The skin under my right eye had become a monstrous terrain, lumpy white areas etched against a fine violet sea. I camouflaged the dark areas, which de-emphasized the contrasting textures, and wasted a great deal of time. For the most part, I saw this particular flaw 'normally,' that is, as a not uncommon minor imperfection which was not disfiguring. But from time to time, it would take over.

The third, and, as it turned out, the last meeting which included Cindy, Doreen and me was at my house. During this meeting, I gave a broad outline of my Disorder, which involved both Body Dysmorphic Disorder and Trichotillomania, and had originally begun with Tourettic Tics and Vocalizations when I was about seven. I told them that they were fortunate that their Disorders were of recent origin and not deeply entrenched. I said I thought it was more than likely that, with the help of medication and therapy, their symptoms would abate.

Retrospective Of First Three Meetings

The first three meetings of my Body-Focused Obsessions and/or Compulsions support group had included Cindy, Doreen, and me. I didn't think Doreen would be coming back. What had happened was that at the last two meetings, Doreen's Obsession with the way her face had changed, and the intensity of her desire for a face lift, had made a powerful impression on me. I was not happy with the way my face had aged, and thought I'd eventually have a face lift, but neither the dissatisfaction, nor the desire to remedy it had reached Obsessive proportions, until I was with Doreen. In other words, I lost my focus. At one point it was total folie a deux. We fantasized about going to Argentina to get face lifts together. Then, when we spoke on the phone and I broke into her plans for a face lift (neither of us could afford one at the time) to remind her that, like me, she had Body Dysmorphic Disorder and should make an effort to refocus when she began to become enmeshed in the Obsession, she screamed at me, accusing me of being a know-it-all. Cindy, I thought, might return, but more likely she'd go to a group which focused exclusively on her Disorder, Trichotillomania.

In retrospect, I see that with respect to Doreen and Cindy, I failed as a facilitator. I suspect it was because my purpose was not clear. I didn't make a distinction between "qualifying": going into as much detail as necessary to describe the Obsessions and Compulsions that brought you to the group, and becoming submerged in the Obsession. The purpose of the support group meeting should be to witness one's

Obsessive thought patterns, not to get lost in them. Another error was losing the focus on the Disorder, and instead using the meeting to have a general conversation about the problems and challenges of our current life situations. I didn't want to prevent people from trying to gain perspective on their lives with the encouragement of a supportive group. But I don't think that ventilating indiscriminately helps to alleviate Obsessive/Compulsive Disorders. The situations and events of our lives and the thoughts and feelings they engender in us should be discussed in reference to how those situations and events, and their mental and emotional residue influence our symptoms, and how the symptoms affect our lives. Most importantly, the emphasis should be on recovery. The meeting should be an opportunity to share whatever works for us in combating the Disorder: psychotherapy, psycho pharmacology, articles, tapes, exercises, affirmations–whatever is enlightening and healing, whatever helps to release us from the grip of our Obsessions and Compulsions.

The Hair Cut

Here a cut, there a cut. I threw out my scissors. The next day, I made two swipes with a razor at the hair level with my right cheekbone. I threw out the razor and began to break the long hair on the right side of the top of my head. It became more and more uneven. It occurred to me that if I had it cut professionally, it might be easier to leave it alone. I'd tried this stratagem before, and it hadn't really worked. What usually happened was that when I pointed out to a hairdresser that he or she was not dealing with the unevenness on the right side, he or she would become defensive and judgmental, and refuse to see what I was referring to, which resulted in my doing endless remedial cutting when I got home. My last professional cut had required only minor remediation, over a period of only three days. In other words, it had helped to end a cycle. What I was hoping for was a hair dresser who could see exactly what I saw, and fix it so I wouldn't have to fix it again—ever. Ha ha!

I found a hairdresser named Vincent, who had a salon on Saint Marks Place. I began to feel it was the right place when Vincent's assistant gave me a pale orange robe to cover my clothes. I usually wear non-colors, black, white, grey, because they're the most flattering. Creamsicle orange is one of the few shades I enjoy wearing. And the fit was perfect. After I'd donned the robe, she washed my hair, making it a great sensual experience unmarred by water splashing on my face. And the cut was the best I'd had since my uncontrollable haircutting began 10 years earlier. I explained that although I liked the top to be longer than the sides, the proportion had become ridiculous. Vincent nodded and said it looked like I was wearing a hat, which I found funny. First he evened out the sides and back to perfection with a razor. Then he began to cut the top from side to side, concentrating on the left side rather than the unevenness on the right side, because the left side was longer, and easier to cut because it was even. Then he stopped to look. I fluffed up my hair. I said that the left side was perfect, and then pointed out the places on the right side that it was poking unattractively up or out . Amazingly, he didn't refuse to see. He cut more in the sections I'd pointed out and said, "mess it up again," which I did. He looked and cut some more. We went through that process a few more times, until we both felt it was done. I left feeling great. When I got home, I noticed sections of hair that I wanted to cut—but not enough to risk being caught up in endless compulsive cutting.

My Reconstituted Support Group

I was half expecting a no-meeting, like the first one I'd planned. I tried to plan a fourth meeting at a time when both Cindy and Doreen could come. As it turned out, the time I'd planned with Cindy wasn't convenient for Doreen. Then, at the last minute, Cindy called, saying she couldn't make it. Instead there were two new women, Rita and Samantha. I'd met Rita at the Obsessive/Compulsive Anonymous meetings, and she'd brought Samantha, whom she'd met at Shelly's Self-Mutilation support group. The two women presented a contrast. Rita was casual; Samantha, dramatic. Samantha spoke mostly about the immanent break-up of her relationship. Her living situation was unbearably insecure, because her boyfriend was paying most of the bills, especially the rent, which was high.

Rita talked about wishing she was glamorous. She said she couldn't look at fashion magazines without going crazy with envy. Strangely, she seemed completely oblivious to Samantha's obvious beauty and glamour. I began to do a mental makeover of Rita. First, I thought, she needed a better haircut, one which would make use of her thick, straight, dark hair in framing her face. Then, since her eyes were her best feature, she should uncover them—get contact lenses and emphasize them with pencil. Then wardrobe: She should stop concealing her small breasts by hunching her shoulders and wearing baggy shirts. Instead, she should wear snug shirts and walk tall. And she should quit wearing sneakers and wear shoes; flat heeled lace up would be OK, as long as they were the fine, not the bulky, type. Rita wasn't a beauty, but she could be strikingly attractive if, instead of trying to camouflage what she thought was wrong, she accepted what she had and worked with her assets. Like me, Rita had a kind of Dysmorphic Disorder linked with a 'make it worse and then camouflage it' Compulsion. In her case it was minor acne eruptions, which she aggravated and then covered with make-up, which consumed inordinate amounts of time and resulted in self-loathing and worse skin.

My Reconstituted Support Group Continues

Rita was at the next meeting, and, in addition, there were two new women, Debbie and Sarah.

I had typed up a list of possible topics for discussion for this meeting, and we discussed some of them.

Rita had suggested "grooming behaviors" as a topic. Since all four of us at this meeting had compulsive, repetitive grooming behaviors, I thought grooming behaviors would be the best subject to begin with. I paraphrased what Judith Rappaport had written, likening Trichotillomania to the grooming behaviors of cats, monkeys, and other mammals, who retreat into grooming behaviors when they find themselves in anxiety-provoking situations. Obviously, these behaviors, picking and smoothing, dissipate anxiety. Think of all of the anxiety-driven grooming that goes on when people are waiting to be interviewed for employment. The problem for us is that we're compelled to repeat these behaviors, whenever we're challenged by the most minimal and/ or routine anxiety, and, even worse, once we start, we can't stop. So, in the long run, these activities provoke more anxiety than they alleviate. No one had anything to add, so I mentioned hypnotherapy, a topic suggested by Sarah, who had tried it.

"Essentially," she said, "it's a process of absorbing positive input to counter your habitual negativities while you're in a highly suggestible state."

When Debbie inquired if hypnosis had worked, Sarah responded ruefully that, yes, it had worked, in the sense that the symptoms she had been most concerned with had disappeared or faded, but that new symptoms had sprung up to take their place. I said that I thought there was value in movement, per se, that personally, I was never as identified with new symptoms as with entrenched ones. Also, the replacement of one symptom by another lets you know with greater certainty that your Disorder has a neurological basis, which alleviates the guilt about "indulging" in it.

Debbie, whose basic Compulsion, like mine, was hair cutting, said that in the past month she'd switched from cutting the hair on her head to cutting pubic hair. She still covered her head completely, including the hairline, because she was a married, orthodox Jewish woman. So we had to take her word that she was letting it grow. I'd noticed that while the older orthodox women in my neighborhood wear wigs, the younger ones frequently substitute soft hats, which cover the entire hair line and fall to the shoulders. Debbie's choice of head covering—a scarf, covered by a hard, shaped hat—was unique in my viewing experience of orthodox Jewish women. Combined with a bathing suit and sarong, it would have the look of a magazine spread advertising vacation wear for the Bahamas. When I put Debbie's uniqueness together with something she said about her shorn pubic hair—that her husband didn't like it, because it was bristly—gave me the feeling that her hair cutting represented a rebellion against her restricted situation, and, at the same time, a capitulation to it.

Sarah came to one more meeting. She was 20 and had been in therapy since childhood, when she first had Obsessive/Compulsive Spectrum Disorder manifestations. She possessed a great deal of knowledge and insight about both the Disorder and its treatment. After she left, I missed her input and her presence. Rita, Debbie, and I continued to meet intermittently over the next several months. We all made progress, if not with the Disorder, then at least with greater self-acceptance, in spite of it.

Diary Selections 1997 and 1998

By the fall of 1997, I had ceased participating in any type of support group, had not been in therapy for some time, and had given up on antidepressants, having tried three of them without much success. Of course, two of them, Wellbutrin and Anafranil, are not the Selective Serotonin Re-uptake Inhibitors recommended for OCD and OCSDs; the third, Prozac, which is the oldest of the SSRIs, was created for depression, rather than anxiety, and to deal with anxiety requires an extremely high dose, a dose which many people (including me) can't tolerate. My Disorder waxed and waned. I no longer gave in to it mindlessly, as I once did; *but I still gave in.* Behaviorally speaking, what's supposed to happen is that when you don't give in, the anxiety passes (that much is true), which makes it easier to resist the next time (false, at least for me). I no longer trusted that sense of urgency, which told me that if I just surrendered this one last time (just check once more, just cut one last hair) it would leave me alone for ever more. The new rationalization was: You might as well surrender now, since sooner or later you will. But why must I? I had accepted a very incomplete recovery. I wasn't overwhelmed by the Disorder; I was limping along with it.

Then, in December of '97, my son Alex told me he was taking Zoloft (sertraline), and it had made an extraordinary difference in his ability to discipline his mind, which in the past had frequently been consumed by Obsessional thinking, the kind of repetitive, intrusive thoughts that the literature on Obsessive/Compulsive Disorder describes. I got a prescription for Zoloft from a GP, who had an understanding of OCD and OCSDs, and knew that these Disorders were commonly treated with SSRIs like Zoloft.

"Mirror, mirror, off the wall, I'm sick and tired of you!" I feel hopeful

12/26/97   I haven't been focused on my face, and my 'need' for a face lift. No strong desire to check on either my face or my hair. I do it inadvertently, out of habit, from time to time, but not for long; I'm not mesmerized.

12/27/97   I finally found the article I was searching for. I'd looked through the same stack three times before, and managed to miss it. What finally occurred was that I mentally let go of it, admitted the possibility that, for some reason, it was no longer in my possession but that I should continue to look, because it probably was there. The lesson is to relinquish the craving for certainty, one of the hallmarks of Obsessive/Compulsive Disorder.

12/28/97   Today, I took my first dose of Zoloft. It seemed to extinguish any concern with my appearance. However, I spent hours at night, first cleaning, but ultimately rearranging the same assortment of decorative chachkas over and over, longing for that feeling of all rightness that would allow me to quit. That need for completion, that perpetually elusive sense of closure, is another facet of OCD and many OCSDs. It's so similar to the need for certainty, that I believe they are related, if not identical.

12/31/98   I spent much of the day struggling with three paragraphs, putting things in, taking things out, recombining and rearranging. I quit to bathe and dress for a New Year's Eve celebration. What a relief! It struck me that my day's activity, the rearrangement of nouns and verbs, conjunctions and commas, had the same quality as my rearrangement of vases and ash trays, coasters and candles, the night before.

1/1/98   The Zoloft is working. Yeah! But, as Alex said, the problem of what to do next is still yours. The drug frees up your time; it doesn't compel you to be constructive or productive. I've set a nondemanding agenda for this evening: eat the rest of Mari's New Year's Eve lasagna while watching TV, wrap gifts for Henry and Peter, and remove the stains from a snugly warm, otherwise wearable white sweater. Happy New Year.

1/3/98   Worry, worry, worry about money is circling around my brain. I'm not having any constructive ideas about it. I decide to go see the Versace exhibit at the Met–last day. It really was the Art of costume. I enjoyed it aesthetically, without ever thinking about wanting to wear any of it. I met Robin and Joe on their way in, as I was leaving. More Happy New Year.

Later that evening I began to write. When I reached a rough spot, I wandered into the bathroom to take a peek in the mirror. Why not, I'd been doing it for 42 years? But this time I'd foiled myself, by covering the mirror with a face towel. So I wandered back to my desk, with its humming, anxiety-provoking computer–waiting for me.

1/4/98   Speaking about the effects of Zoloft, Alex said, "I feel fluorescent," followed by an electrical sounding, "zzzzzzzzzzzz."

I felt the same way. Only I liked it, because it came with a sensation of silliness. This effect lasted for only a week. Actually, for two days in the middle of the first week, part of the Disorder, the impulse control,

Trichotillomaniac aspect was accentuated. It was as if my fingers were magnetically pulled to my head. I couldn't disengage them long enough to turn on the TV. Fortunately, that didn't last.

1/6/98   I've been sleeping a lot. I think it's partly the medication; I've heard it can have that effect. But I feel it's largely psychological: the feeling of emptiness. What do I do now, after decades of filling in so much of the time with Dysmorphic Obsessions and Compulsions?

1/12/98   I've had the habit of eating one real meal a day, supplemented by fruit and sweets before and after. I've already learned that with Zoloft if I eat too much, too fast, at one sitting, I become drowsy. But I did it again: slept from 10 pm till midnight and spent the next several hours anxiously wondering if I would be able to fall asleep again. I did a lot of pacing, turning on and off the TV, picking up and putting down books and magazines–but no hair checking, either visual or manual.

1/14/98   I'm experiencing the 'Selective Serotonin Re-uptake Inhibitor as water-wings' effect, that Dr. Jeffrey M. Schwartz talks about in *Brainlock*. Aloft with Zoloft! I still find myself in front of the mirror from time to time, stretching out hairs, looking for the one that "needs" to be broken or cut. But I don't get stuck. Within a minute or two, I see what I'm doing from a detached perspective. It's not necessary; so I stop. The SSRI doesn't force you to refrain from doing the behavior, but it lessens the emotional attachment to the Obsessional element. My hair is still uneven, but I can live with it. So now I have to decide what to do next.

Cognitive/Behavioral Therapy, the type of Therapy recommended for Obsessive/Compulsive Spectrum Disorders, involves a mindful awareness of what one is actually thinking and doing. Dr. Schwartz's Cognitive/Behavioral model differs from others I've encountered, in that the emphasis is on "refocusing," finding something constructive with which to occupy one's self.

1/18/98   Yesterday, I accidentally took a double dose of Zoloft. I awoke from a disturbing dream, in which I was being chased. I hadn't fully shaken it off when I took the first 100 mg. pill, absentmindedly. Then, not remembering I'd taken one, I swallowed another soon after. I became extremely chilled. All of my muscles were clenched against the cold, and every minor pain or discomfort was magnified. I knew that in order to warm up, I needed to get moving, but it was hours before I could mobilize myself. I realized then that Zoloft is powerful medication.

1/20/98   Zoloft has arrested my Obsessions and Compulsions for the time being. But it hasn't cured paralyzing anxiety. I sill resist going to sleep at an hour that would enable me to enjoy the next day and use it constructively. It feels odd to be free of compelling symptoms, when I'm too anxious to either sleep or act. It's now become painfully clear that I have to decide what to do. I can no longer evade action by default, exhausting myself in Obsessions and Compulsions. The drug allows for more mindful awareness, for observing what my mind is dipping into, which gives me an opportunity to change its direction.

1/23/98   Alex said the Zoloft wasn't working for him anymore: his Obsession has returned. I reminded him of the part of *Brainlock* where it says that the Obsessions do come back, but that they're less compelling. He said that was true, that he didn't really care as much about the content of the Obsession. We talked about distinguishing between what a drug can reasonably be expected to do for you, and what you have to do for yourself.

1/29/98   3 am   My sleep pattern is still perverse. I can't sleep at night because I've slept all day, and I can't get up in the morning because I was up all night, and on and on. So I haven't been doing very much substitute teaching. Instead, I've been beating myself up about not working, and worrying about money. Down, down, down, and then, not surprisingly, I began checking, both visually and manually for hairs that "should" be cut. I snapped out of it after about 15 minutes, without cutting or breaking any hairs. It happened four times today, each time for a slightly longer duration before becoming aware of what I was doing. And each time, in that moment of realization, I had the sensation of being an absurdly programmed robot. Why did the drug fail to block my Obsessive Compulsive urges today, as it has for a month now? I think that once I became enmeshed in self-castigation and worry, it was easy for the familiar Obsessions and Compulsions to slip back in. My honeymoon with Zoloft is over. The drug can make it easier to discipline my mind, but won't do the trick for me.

1/31/98   My mind skipped from one anxious rumination to another. What would I do today?

I decided to go to the library, where I looked up the three drugs I've taken in an effort to combat my Disorder, in *The Essential Guide To Prescription Drugs*, by James J. Rybacki, Pharmacist, and James W. Long, *M.D.*. It was here that I discovered that Wellbutrin (bupropion) works on the two nerve transmitters, norepinephrine and dopamine, and not on serotonin, the neurotransmitter that all of the literature says is implicated in OCD and OCSDs. I can't imagine why Dr. Laakso prescribed it for me! Wellbutrin seems to be a mood elevator. In any case, I'd given up on it after a couple of days, because of my dry mouth and overmedicated feeling, even at low dosages.

Next I looked up Zoloft (sertraline), which has been working well both for me and my son. I was dismayed when I read under the "possible, but not probable side effects: hemorrhaging into the anterior chamber of the eye! A psychiatrist told me the hemorrhaging was probably due to the blood thinning effect of Zoloft. *The Essential Guide* also stated that the drug had caused delayed bone development in the fetuses of laboratory animals. This should be widely publicized, to avoid another "Thalidomide" disaster.

Prozac (fluoxetine) has a relatively good side effect profile. Yet it hadn't worked for me, because the dosage required to handle anxiety is too high. I decided to investigate the other two Serotonin Re-uptake Inhibitors, Paxil (paroxetine) and Luvox (fluvoxamine), which had become available in '93 and '95, respectively.

Paxil is recommended for Panic Attacks, as well as for Depression and OCD. I decided it was not for me, for two reasons. Under "normal expected side effects," it mentions lowered blood pressure to the point of fainting upon standing up. My blood pressure is already low. And in the "possible, but not probable" category, it mentions dehydration with dry mouth, which I already have a tendency toward. The dehydrated feeling was one of the reasons for my being unable to tolerate either Wellbutrin or the higher dosages of Prozac recommended for OCD. However, because Paxil is recommended for Panic Disorder, it would be my drug of choice, in spite of the drawbacks, if I were suffering from recurrent panic attacks, as I did at the age of 19. At that time, the only drugs available for treating panic attack were 'knock you over the head' tranquilizers. I also think Paxil should probably be the first SSRI tried by pre-menopausal women, because it has the best pregnancy profile—"no changes in fetuses of laboratory animals given ten times the dose normally prescribed for humans." Actually, I suggest that anyone considering taking an SSRI research it in *The Essential Guide To Prescription Drugs,* since there is no "best one" for everyone.

All of these drugs are contraindicated for Bipolar Disorder, because they can provoke an onset of the manic phase. Also SSRIs and Lithium (frequently prescribed for people with Bi-polar Disorder) shouldn't be used in combination. As for minor side effects, all of the SSRIs cause a fairly high percentage of users to experience sexual dysfunction and/or loss of libido.

Luvox is the only SSRI which lists depression as a secondary use, rather than a primary one. Evidently, it was developed primarily for OCD. It has also been found to be useful in the treatment of Binge Eating and Compulsive Exhibitionism. These are Impulse Control Disorders, so it should be useful in the treatment of Trichotillomania, though this is not listed. It is also supposed to be helpful in the treatment of Tension Headaches. All in all, Luvox seems to be geared to alleviating High Anxiety, rather than Depression. It might be even better for me than Zoloft. The only contraindication for me is that "somnolence" is listed in the "possible, but not probable" side effects category, and somnolence is precisely the problem I'm having with Zoloft, which includes "drowsiness and fatigue" among the possible but not probable side effects. In fact, I'm not sure to what extent the somnolence is due to the drug. I mean, when large chunks of time that used to be claimed by Obsessive/Compulsive concerns and demands are freed up, there's a lot of "what should I do now?" Anxiety. And the easiest way out is sleep.

Awakening

I've used either Zoloft or Luvox most of the time over the past four years. I switch back and forth because each seems to become ineffective after several months, while the one I haven't been taking is effective once more. My son Alex who'd used Paxil for a couple of years said that the drug had become ineffective for him. I told him that it was not uncommon for the body to become tolerant of a particular SSRI, and that all that was needed was to switch to another. He had tried Zoloft and hadn't like it, so I suggested he try Luvox, which was working well for me. He tried it, and reported that after two days, his forehead had become freckled for the first time. It occurred to me that the unattractive dark spots on my face that I'd aquired over the past four years were probably the result of Luvox making my skin particularly sensitive to sunlight. I stopped using it and went back to Zoloft. I've also tried Paxil, which made me feel lethargic and unmotivated. So if Zoloft stops working I may try Celexa (Citalopram), another SSRI, which has been used in the US only since 1998, but has been used in Europe since 1989.

How well does the SSRI–Luvox or Zoloft–control the Disorder? Well, as I stated earlier, an SSRI can only do so much; you have to do the rest yourself. And, sorry to say, I still cut and break hair. At the moment, my hair is long in front and short in back. It looks kind of punk. But more important to me than the appearance of my hair is being in control of my time. And, with respect to time spent on my Disorder, there has been a major shift, due partly to my current SSRI and partly to my understanding of my Disorder. I am no longer late either to work or to social engagements because of my Disorder; and that is a great, hard-won freedom. It now takes me about half an hour to get my face and hair together in the morning. I am no longer captive of the mirror for endless hours. Later in the day, in the evening, for example, I frequently find my hands in my hair. Most of the time, I can stop when I become aware of what I am doing. Occasionally, when I'm really stressed out about something, I'll start breaking or cutting hair, before I'm consciously aware I've what I'm doing–clearly a symptom of Trichotillomania. The Body Dysmorphic aspect of my Disorder has been much ameliorated. In fact, it is not sufficiently time consuming to be considered clinically significant.

I know that the SSRI "works", because when I go off it for a few days, I always become involved in either hair cutting or in endless ruminations about minor facial flaws. Unfortunately, when I go back on the antidepressant, for the first day it has an effect opposite to the one intended: it intensifies the symptoms of the Disorder. Is this "*As Good As It Gets*," to quote the movie (title and dialogue) whose protagonist has OCD? I don't know. From time to time I retreat into the monomaniacal focus which is the essence of my Disorder. But, much more frequently, I transcend it.

0-595-26254-6

Don't go to
get my
hair cut
any more:

too embarrassing

when they ask

who did

Printed in the United States
24774LVS00005B/9